Beyond the School Doors

The Literacy Needs of Job Seekers Served by the U.S. Department of Labor

Irwin S. Kirsch
•
Ann Jungeblut
•
Anne Campbell

September 1992

U.S. Department of Labor • Employment and Training Administration

 Educational Testing Service

ISBN: 0-88685-136-X

The work upon which this publication is based was performed pursuant to Contract No. 99-8-3458-75-052-01 of the Department of Labor. It does not, however, necessarily reflect the views of that agency.

v   **Foreword**

1   **Section 1: Overview and Highlights**

     1   Setting a Context

     3   The Literacy Assessment

     5   The JTPA and ES/UI Programs

     6   Highlights from this Assessment

     10   About this Report

13   **Section 2: Defining and Profiling Levels of Proficiency**

     16   Prose Literacy
         Characterizing Proficiency Levels on the Prose Scale
         Profiling Proficiencies on the Prose Scale

     31   Document Literacy
         Characterizing Proficiency Levels on the Document Scale
         Profiling Proficiencies on the Document Scale

     50   Quantitative Literacy
         Characterizing Proficiency Levels on the Quantitative Scale
         Profiling Proficiencies on the Quantitative Scale
         Summary and Conclusions

65   **Section 3: Comparing Literacy Proficiencies**

     65   Total JTPA and ES/UI Populations

     66   Men and Women

     66   Age

     67   Race/Ethnicity

     69   Levels of Education

     73   Employment, Earnings, and Occupation

     79   Summary

81   Section 4:   **Characterizing Educational Experiences of JTPA and ES/UI Populations**

      82   Literacy Materials in the Home

      83   Work Experiences While in High School

      83   Highest Grade of School Completed

      86   Reason Given For Not Completing High School

      88   Studying for and Receiving a GED

      90   Summary

93   Section 5:   **Characterizing Activities and Perceptions of JTPA and ES/UI Populations**

      94   Civic Experiences

      99   Current Literacy Activities

      103 Self-Perceptions about Literacy Skills

      109 Summary

113 Section 6:   **Implications for New Directions**

119   **Acknowledgments**

120   **Project Staff**

Foreword

The findings of this report underscore how far we have to go to meet the President's and Governors' National Goal for the Year 2000, that "every American will be literate and will possess the knowledge and skills necessary to compete in a global economy. . . ." This comprehensive literacy assessment — dealing with prose, document, and quantitative tasks — provides results that profile a national sample of nearly 20 million participants in the U.S. Department of Labor programs that target people who are unemployed and seeking work or those in search of better jobs. The programs comprise by far the largest component of Labor's Employment and Training Administration activities.

The principal finding from this literacy assessment is that a substantial proportion of these workers and job seekers have minimal literacy skills. Even the 25 to 40 percent who are at the next highest level have skills that are often inadequate for career mobility or advancement. In all, about half a million JTPA trainees and 7.6 million people receiving Unemployment Insurance or services of the Employment Service have literacy skills insufficient for today's jobs.

This literacy survey is the first such comprehensive assessment of these workers and job seekers. It was carried out by Educational Testing Service under contract with the Employment and Training Administration. *Profiling the Literacy Proficiencies of JTPA and ES/UI Populations* and the report prepared for the general public, *Beyond the School Doors*, reflect an effort to measure information-processing skills in three areas key to the day-to-day management of one's life:

- **prose comprehension** skills, such as those a voter might employ to understand editorials on complex civic issues
- **document literacy** skills, such as those a patient might need to decipher charts and tables showing health benefits
- **quantitative** skills, like those a customer might apply in filling out an order form or managing a checking account

The Employment and Training Administration will use this three-dimensional assessment in its efforts to improve the literacy of participants in all its programs. This survey (and new literacy tests now under development) also may heighten Americans' awareness of the critical need to invest in human capital in order to strengthen our economic viability. We also believe the reports will serve to inform related literacy assessment efforts throughout the nation and will buttress the development of human resource policies the nation requires to retain its competitiveness in the year 2000 and beyond.

Roberts T. Jones
Assistant Secretary of Labor
for Employment and
Training Administration

SECTION 1

OVERVIEW AND HIGHLIGHTS

What remains of the old industrial base are mostly printing companies, metalworking plants, and food processors — Where manufacturing provided 36 percent of all employment as recently as 1960, it accounts for only one job in five now. Instead jobs in banking, insurance, and other aspects of finance have opened for the middle class; those whose lack of education would once have restricted them to factory work must now resort to jobs in less lucrative service industries. The Chicago that Sandburg called "Tool Maker, Stacker of Wheat" is increasingly the city of the broker and the data processor on the one hand and the hotel maid on the other.

(From "Chicago: Welcome to the Neighborhood" by Richard Conniff in National Geographic, 179, 5, May 1991, p. 54)

Can America's current education and training systems keep pace with our society's rapid technological, economic, and labor market changes? Concern over this question led the Employment and Training Administration (ETA) within the United States Department of Labor (DOL) to award Educational Testing Service (ETS) a contract to assess the literacy skills of Job Training Partnership Act and Employment Service/Unemployment Insurance program participants. This report summarizes the results obtained from an individually administered literacy assessment of nearly 6,000 adults representing some 20 million persons participating in these DOL programs. Together, these two programs provide services to a significant proportion of America's job seekers — those looking either to enter or reenter the work force, or those looking to improve their status by obtaining a (better) job. In an effort to understand better the need for such a literacy study and how the results may be useful to policymakers and program providers, it will be helpful to place this assessment into a broader social and political context.

● SETTING A CONTEXT

As a nation, we have put a high premium on literacy skills as they affect both individual well-being and society at large. During the last century, literacy took on even greater importance as we moved from predominantly an agrarian to an industrial society. It was during this transition that our nation required increasing numbers of individuals to possess a core set of skills and knowledge in order to meet changing societal needs. The introduction of compulsory schooling served to meet this requirement, and literacy became the primary tool for learning.

As part of his plan for the University of Virginia, Thomas Jefferson defined three objectives for education:

- to prepare some citizens to be public leaders;

- to enable all citizens to exercise the rights of self-government; and,

- to prepare all citizens for the pursuit of happiness.

Education that fulfills these objectives will vary according to a country's stage of development. The types and levels of literacy skills necessary for economic participation, citizenship, and individual advancement in 1800 are different from those required in 1900, which, in turn, are different from those skills that will be important in the year 2000. We live in a technologically advancing society, where both the number and types of written materials are growing and where increasing numbers of citizens are expected to use this information in new and more complex ways.

Within this context, historians[1] remind us that during the last 200 years, our nation's literacy skills have increased dramatically in response to these new requirements and expanded opportunities for social and economic growth. There have also been periods when demands seemed to surpass levels of attainment. Whenever these periods occurred, we have tended to point to the failure of our educational system and to warn of serious social and economic consequences. Today, although we are a better educated and more literate society than at any other time in our history, we find ourselves in one of these periods of imbalance. Whereas in the past we relied primarily on our formal education system to correct any imbalance that existed, we now recognize that this school-centered strategy can be only part of the solution.

Rapid technological, economic, and labor market changes demand that we pay increasing attention to the skill deficiencies of those already in the work force. It is estimated that almost 80 percent of the projected work force for the year 2000 are already employed. As a result, it is now widely recognized that developing new and better strategies to increase the literacy levels of both the current as well as the future work force is essential if our nation is to maintain its standard of living and to compete successfully in global markets. Increased literacy levels are equally important for participation in our mass technological society with its formal institutions,

---

[1] C. F. Kaestle, H. Damon-Moore, L. C. Stedman, K. Tinsley, and W. V. Trollinger, Jr. (1991). *Literacy in the United States: Readers and reading since 1880.* (New Haven, CT: Yale University Press.)

complex legal system, and large government programs. Our future social and economic well-being depends on our ability to meet this challenge.

At the historic 1989 education summit in Charlottesville, Virginia, President Bush and the governors set out to establish a set of national education goals that would guide America into the twenty-first century. As adopted and reported by members of the National Governors' Association, one of the six goals states:

> *By the year 2000, every adult American will be literate and will possess the knowledge and skills necessary to compete in a global economy and exercise the rights and responsibilities of citizenship.*

While our nation's concern with literacy appropriately encompasses all areas of life, much attention in recent years has been focused on workplace literacy skills, particularly in light of what many observers believe is a new social and political era in the United States. Along with the belief that the United States has entered into a new era, is the concern of many policymakers and analysts that the education and training system in this country is not adequate to play its expected role in ensuring individual opportunity, in increasing productivity, and in strengthening America's competitiveness in a global economy.[2] This report goes to the heart of the current debate by focusing on the nature and extent of literacy problems facing America's job seekers and the need to increase the value of America's human capital.

● The Literacy Assessment

The initial step in launching the DOL assessment was to consider the adoption of an operational definition of literacy that would become the basis for setting assessment objectives and a blueprint for developing new tasks to simulate the use of printed materials across adult contexts. Consensus was reached by an external committee of researchers, practitioners, and policymakers to adopt the definition and framework for literacy developed for the 1985 young adult literacy assessment. As presented in the report of that assessment,[3] literacy was defined as:

> **Using printed and written information to function in society, to achieve one's goals, and to develop one's knowledge and potential. (p. 3)**

---

[2] T. Bailey. (November, 1989). *Changes in the nature and structure of work: Implications for skill requirements and skill formation.* (New York: National Center on Education and Employment.)

[3] I. S. Kirsch and A. Jungeblut. (1986). *Literacy: Profiles of America's young adults.* (NAEP Report No. 16-PL-01), (Princeton, NJ: Educational Testing Service.)

Inherent in this definition are two important assumptions. The first is the rejection of an arbitrary standard for literacy — such as signing one's name, the completion of five years of schooling, or the achievement of an eighth-grade level on a standardized test of reading — that can be selected to separate the "literate" from the "illiterate." Second, it implies a set of complex information-processing skills that goes beyond decoding and comprehending school-like texts.

Earlier work with the young adult literacy assessment and ongoing research at ETS has resulted in a set of procedures that have proven useful in the analyses of existing literacy items as well as in the development of new simulation tasks. Building on this work, the DOL assessment incorporated the following types of literacy tasks developed from the kinds of materials adults frequently encounter: **prose tasks** involving reading newspaper articles, editorials, and, stories; **document tasks** based on job applications, payroll schedules, and maps; and basic mathematics or **quantitative tasks** involving a bank deposit slip, order form, and an advertisement for a loan. Such frequently occurring tasks were purposely chosen to simulate the range of literacy tasks adults face every day at work, at home, and in their communities. The pool of simulation tasks included those used in 1985 with a nationally representative sample of 21- to 25-year-olds and tasks newly developed for the DOL assessment — for a total of some 180 tasks. The original tasks provided a necessary link to the young adult literacy assessment, while the newly developed tasks helped to refine and extend the three literacy domains.

No single participant in the DOL survey could be expected to respond to the entire set of simulation tasks given the 60 minutes allowed for administration of the simulation tasks. It was necessary, therefore, to adopt a procedure by which each individual would respond to a subset of literacy tasks, while at the same time ensuring that the total set of tasks was administered across nationally representative samples of each DOL population. Literacy tasks were placed into blocks or sections that were then compiled into booklets of three blocks each in such a way that each block appears in each position and each block is paired with every other block. For this assessment, 13 blocks of tasks were assembled into 26 different assessment booklets, each of which contained a unique combination of three blocks. In a one-on-one interview, each participant in the DOL assessment responded to literacy tasks in only one booklet.

In addition to the time allocated for administration of the simulation tasks, 20 minutes were also devoted to obtaining background information that could be related to demonstrated performance. Major areas explored included: **background and demographics**, i.e., country of birth, home environment including languages spoken or read, accessibility of reading materials, size of household, educational attainment of parents, age, race/ethnicity, service in the armed forces, and marital status; **education**, i.e., highest grade completed in school, current aspirations, participation in GED or ABE classes, and types of training or education received outside public schooling; **labor market experiences**, i.e., employment status, recent labor market experiences, and occupation; **income**, i.e., personal and household; and, **activities**, i.e., voting behavior, hours spent watching television, frequency and content of newspaper reading, and use of literacy on the job.

The information obtained from these interviews is compiled on a data tape that is available to the public as is the full Final Report[4] of this assessment that presents a more thorough discussion of the design, conduct, findings, and conclusions than does this document. This national database provides the most complete picture of the literacy skills and practices of a nationally representative sample of Job Training Partnership Act (JTPA) eligible applicants and Employment Service/Unemployment Insurance (ES/UI) participants.

• THE JTPA AND ES/UI PROGRAMS

ETA is the training and employment security agency of the Department of Labor. It oversees, among others, the federally mandated training and job service programs of the Job Training Partnership Act, the various job service activities of the U.S. Employment Service, and the income security program of the Unemployment Insurance Service. These programs represent major facets of the public policy on human resources and comprise by far the largest component of ETA's activities.

The Job Training Partnership Act. The Job Training Partnership Act of 1982 was initiated in October of 1983. Its objective is to bring the jobless into permanent, unsubsidized, and self-sustaining employment by providing training, basic education, job counseling, and placement. The target populations of various programs include economically disadvantaged adults and youths, dislocated workers, and other groups who face serious employment barriers. Thus, the composition of the JTPA client population is quite varied and includes experienced workers, new entrants and reentrants to the work force, young and older workers, and workers associated with regular and permanent employment, as well as those whose employment tends to be seasonal or irregular. The common thread among these diverse candidates for JTPA services is a persistent difficulty in finding jobs. The JTPA program aims to ameliorate

---

[4] I. S. Kirsch and A. Jungeblut. (1992). *Profiling the literacy proficiencies of JTPA and ES/UI populations: Final report to the Department of Labor.* (Princeton, NJ: Educational Testing Service.)

this difficulty through training, remedial education, and various types of job services. Although the mix of services differs from site to site, JTPA programs typically include three elements — basic educational activities, occupational skills training, and job placement services. The educational component can include both remedial education and preparation for the General Education Development (GED) examination.

The Employment Service/Unemployment Insurance Programs. The Wagner-Peyser Act of 1933, as amended in 1982, established the jointly financed federal-state system of public employment services. Under this law, states are provided funds to operate labor exchange systems that respond to the specific conditions of each state and meet the demands of its employers and workers. Operated through state employment security agencies, the mission of the U.S. Employment Service (ES) includes: assisting job seekers in finding employment commensurate with their skill levels; assisting employers in filling job vacancies with workers who meet the job requirements; providing interstate job-market clearance through exchange of information on labor market conditions; assisting the unemployment insurance system in ensuring that beneficiaries meet the "work test" (whereby the "ability and availability" to work as a condition for unemployment insurance eligibility is demonstrated); and, providing job-counseling services to handicapped persons and others. To operate this system, some 2,000 local employment service offices are maintained.

The present Unemployment Insurance (UI) program was created by the Social Security Act of 1935 to provide temporary income protection for involuntarily unemployed workers. While the specific benefit provisions vary among states, the weekly benefits typically replace about 50 percent of lost wages over a 26-week period for most recipients, with this period extended at times of very high unemployment. Depending on individual state requirements, eligibility for UI benefits is based on a particular amount of money earned or on weeks worked one year prior to filing a claim. All state unemployment insurance laws require that a person be both able and available to work in order to receive unemployment benefits; registration for work at a public employment office is regarded as evidence of such "ability and availability." As a result, a large proportion of the ES applicant group consists of UI recipients.

● *Highlights from this Assessment*

In reporting the results, the DOL assessment follows a profile approach[5] that views literacy not as a single dimension along which a single cutpoint

---

[5] I. S. Kirsch. (1990). "Measuring adult literacy." In *Toward defining literacy*, edited by R. L. Venezky, D. A. Wagner, and B. S. Ciliberti. (Newark, DE: International Reading Association.)

or standard can be selected to separate the "literate" from the "illiterate," but in terms of three scales representing distinct and important aspects of literacy:

Prose literacy: the knowledge and skills associated with understanding and using information from texts such as editorials, newspaper articles, stories, poems, and the like.

Document literacy: the knowledge and skills associated with locating and using information in tables, charts, graphs, maps, indexes, and so forth.

Quantitative literacy: the knowledge and skills associated with performing different arithmetic operations, either alone or sequentially, using information embedded in both prose and document materials.

This approach seems particularly useful for assessing literacy proficiencies relevant to the workplace since it focuses on the application of skills in situations that adults need to cope with on a regular basis. This DOL assessment goes beyond the earlier young adult literacy assessment by identifying five levels of literacy proficiency and the associated information-processing skills required for successful performance at each level on the prose, document, and quantitative scales.

Not surprisingly, the tasks become more demanding and the associated skills increasingly more complex as the reader moves up the literacy scales from Level 1 to Level 5. (See Section 2 of this report for a description of these levels.) In combination with a set of broad demographic and background variables — i.e., gender, age, race/ethnicity, educational attainment, and employment history — these literacy levels along with average proficiency scores provide a useful way to characterize the JTPA and ES/UI populations. The major findings and conclusions from this assessment are highlighted below.

Findings:

- Individuals in the DOL programs who demonstrate higher levels of literacy skills tend to avoid long periods of unemployment, earn higher wages, and work in higher level occupations than those program participants who demonstrate lower literacy skills.

- On average, demonstrated literacy skills differ considerably on each of the three literacy scales among those reporting various occupations. In fact, the range of average proficiency scores extends almost a full standard deviation or 50 points.

- Some 65 and 60 percent of the JTPA and ES/UI client groups, respectively, perceive that they could get a (better) job if their reading or writing skills were improved and roughly 80 and 70 percent, respectively, report that their job opportunities would improve with increased skill in mathematics.

- On each of the three literacy scales, some 40 to 50 percent of the eligible JTPA applicants and roughly 40 percent of the ES/UI program participants demonstrate literacy skills in Levels 1 and 2, the lowest two of the five defined levels. At these levels, tasks require relatively low-level information-processing skills, and it seems likely that skills evident at these levels would place severe restrictions on full participation in our increasingly complex society, including the workplace.

- About 15 to 20 percent of the JTPA and 20 to 25 percent of the ES/UI population demonstrate proficiencies defined by the highest two levels, Levels 4 and 5. For the most part, individuals scoring at these two levels demonstrate proficiencies in coping with complex printed or written material whether in prose or document format or proficiencies that require the application of two or more sequential arithmetic operations. Other things being equal, these individuals appear to be an untapped resource.

- Contrary to other national databases, the DOL data indicate that Black and Hispanic JTPA and ES/UI populations are not statistically different from each other in terms of their average proficiency scores on the three scales. They are each disproportionately represented, however, at the low and high levels on the literacy scales when compared with White respondents. Some 50 to 60 percent of the Black and Hispanic populations are represented at Levels 1 and 2 compared with 25 to 30 percent of the White populations. In contrast, only 8 to 12 percent of Black and Hispanic JTPA and ES/UI participants attain Levels 4 and 5 compared with 25 to 40 percent of the White program participants.

- About 75 to 95 percent of program participants with zero to eight years of education and 65 to 70 percent of those with nine to 12 years of education but no high school diploma score in the lowest two levels on each of the three literacy scales. Of particular concern is the fact that a substantial percentage of individuals who report earning a high school diploma or GED demonstrate very limited skills. That is, some 35 to 45 percent of JTPA and ES/UI participants who report this level of education are estimated to have literacy skills limited to Levels 1 and 2.

- Demonstrated literacy skills seem to be associated with pursuing and obtaining the GED. Among both the JTPA and ES/UI populations, those individuals without a high school diploma who demonstrate higher literacy skills are more likely to report having studied for the GED than those demonstrating lower skill levels. Moreover, among those studying for the GED, the difference in average proficiency scores ranges from 35 to 50 points on a 500-point scale in favor of those who attain the certificate over those who report studying for the GED but not obtaining it.

- The demonstrated literacy proficiencies of GED certificate holders are similar to the proficiencies of high school graduates in both DOL populations.

Conclusions:

- Given the diversity of our national population and the fact that the high school diploma apparently no longer certifies a set of literacy competencies, outcome measures are needed that ensure comparability across individuals and time periods. Examples of some existing programs that use national measures ensuring comparability are the SAT and ACT for college admissions and the ASVAB for military placement. What policymakers and business leaders appear to be seeking are integrated information systems that combine background and assessment data that will yield information that can be useful at the program, state, and national levels. Any such system will need to be applicable to diverse adult populations making the transition from school to work or from job to job.

- If demonstrated literacy skills continue to be used as an important indicator of our nation's human resource capability, then it is necessary that we learn more about the literacy requirements of key job families or related occupations.

- The findings of this assessment clearly show that large proportions from each of the two DOL populations surveyed demonstrate very limited literacy skills — that is, on each of the three literacy scales 40 to 50 percent of the eligible JTPA applicants and ES/UI participants demonstrate skills that fall within the ranges defined here as Level 1 and Level 2. Unless an attempt is made to upgrade the level of literacy skills of these individuals, their success in job training programs may be limited, thus denying them access to the job market. Moreover, for those individuals who do succeed in a job training program without a concomitant increase in their literacy skills, the question remains whether a demonstrated low level of proficiency will enable them to avoid future employment difficulties that may arise from projected increases in skill requirements.

- Literacy education and training practices must be broadened both within the traditional K-12 school program as well as in continuing education and training programs by focusing on literacy skills associated with the full range of printed or written materials from various adult contexts. This is necessary not only because schools are producing future generations of workers but also because the school model for reading instruction — the model that has resulted in large proportions of adults demonstrating limited literacy skills — is prevalent in many workplace and community education programs. The question is how should existing instructional practices be changed — both behind and beyond the school doors.

- Projected changes in the workplace coupled with the fact that 40 to 50 percent of the JTPA and ES/UI populations score in the range defined by Levels 1 and 2 suggest that there is a significant need for adult education programs. The fact that some 60 to 80 percent of the DOL client groups perceive that they could get a better job with improved skills suggests that, at this time and for the foreseeable future, there will be increasing pressure on adult education and training programs to provide relevant services for individuals demonstrating low-level literacy skills.

- The findings of this and earlier assessments clearly indicate that independent of other salient demographic and background variables, engaging in various reading and writing activities is a good predictor of higher literacy proficiencies. To facilitate long-term solutions to the literacy problems facing our adult population, steps must be taken to ensure that literacy and literacy practices come to be more universally valued by our citizens.

• ABOUT THIS REPORT

Between November 1989 and June 1990, nationally representative random samples of 2,501 eligible JTPA applicants in 14 states and 3,277 ES/UI participants in 16 states responded to a set of background questions and an assessment booklet with, on average, some 40 literacy tasks. These instruments were administered by ETS-trained JTPA and state agency office staff during face-to-face interviews lasting approximately 90 minutes. This report describes and compares the demonstrated literacy proficiencies of both client groups served by the Employment and Training Administration within the United States Department of Labor.

Because the proportions of adults assessed in these two populations are based on weighted samples — rather than on the entire populations — the numbers reported in tables throughout this report are estimates. As such, they are subject to a measure of uncertainty that is characterized by a statistic known as the standard error of estimate. Comparisons discussed in this report are based on statistical tests that consider both the magnitude of the observed difference and the size of the standard errors associated with the observations. A significance level of .05 was used to determine whether two groups or two proportions were statistically different from each other.[6] The reader is advised to rely on the results of statistical tests rather than on the apparent magnitude of any observed difference to determine whether the differences are likely to represent actual or "true" differences.

The major results highlighted in this section are discussed in more detail throughout the remainder of this report. Section 2 describes the percentages of adults who demonstrate proficiency in the five defined levels for each of three literacy scales. In addition, each level of each scale is described in terms of the information-processing requirements associated with successful performance at that level. Section 3 examines and compares the average proficiency of various subpopulations within the JTPA and ES/UI client groups. Section 4 characterizes the two DOL populations with respect to educational experiences that are related to their high school years. Section 5 also focuses on background characteristics, namely on activities and perceptions related to literacy. Section 6 is a short reflection by the authors on the DOL study and some of the implications of these findings.

Placed in perspective, this report, the more detailed Final Report, and the public-use data tape comprise a rich and unique set of information that may be used to inform policy debates and set program agenda for both the JTPA and the ES/UI client groups. It also provides a baseline of information from which to measure changes over time and from which to compare other subpopulations within America.

---

[6] Unless otherwise noted, any significant differences referred to in this report are significant at the .05 level or greater. Statistically significant differences can be tested using a standard t-test $\dfrac{x_1 - x_2}{\sqrt{(SE_1)^2 + (SE_2)^2}}$.

DEFINING AND
PROFILING LEVELS
OF PROFICIENCY

*T*he focus of this section of the report is on extending the process of conceptualizing and anchoring the prose, document, and quantitative literacy scales that were originally established as part of the literacy assessment of young adults. In reading through this section, it is important to recognize that the tasks designed to measure each literacy area represent a variety of purposes people have for using printed or written information as well as a variety of materials associated with these uses. This framework was applied because it takes into account the fact that performance on a given task depends to a large degree on what is read (material) and what the respondent is asked to do with the material (question/ directive).

Each of the literacy scales is designed to range from 0 to 500. Experience indicates, however, that the majority of tasks fall between 200 and 400 on each scale. Tasks from each of the three literacy scales are placed on their respective scale based on a correct response probability (RP) criterion of 80 percent (RP80). A complete list of all tasks by scale and RP80 value is provided in the Final Report. The aim here is to guide appropriate interpretation of RP80 values at various levels of proficiency along each scale. Table 2.1 provides a brief description of selected prose literacy tasks, their RP80 values, and the associated probabilities of responding correctly at various proficiency levels. As reflected in this table, it is important to recognize that the model used to generate these data places both tasks and people on the appropriate literacy scale. Although the examples and the interpretations made here apply to the prose literacy scale, performance data on the other two scales are interpreted in the same manner.

To help us understand what this means, consider someone who is performing at the 250 level on the prose scale. The information in Table 2.1 shows that such an individual can be expected to perform tasks at about this level with 80 percent probability — that is, to perform eight out of 10 tasks at the 250 level correctly. In other words, such an individual would be expected to respond successfully to this task and others like it in a very consistent manner. An individual performing at the 250 level has an 82 percent chance of responding correctly to the 246-level task involving a magazine article. In addition, this table shows that this individual would have even higher probabilities of success performing easier tasks. A person at the 250 level would be expected to perform tasks at about the 200 level with more than a 90 percent probability, e.g., that person has a 94 percent probability of success performing the 209-level task listed in Table 2.1.

| Table 2.1 | Selected Tasks and Associated Probabilities Along the Prose Scale |

Description of Selected Tasks	RP80 Value	Associated Probabilities at Selected Proficiency Levels						
		150	200	250	300	350	400	450
Identify single piece of information in a brief sports article	209	36	75	94	99	100	100	100
Identify single piece of information in a short announcement	210	40	75	93	98	100	100	100
Locate information in lengthy magazine article	246	11	43	82	97	99	100	100
Match two features of information in a brief sports article	253	13	42	78	95	99	100	100
Rephrase information stated in a magazine article	298	1	7	36	82	97	100	100
Integrate information from a news article on the economy	305	4	15	44	78	94	99	100
Compare new and old ways of processing credit card charges	346	3	10	28	57	82	94	98
Identify two situations that satisfy a given criterion	356	2	7	21	49	77	92	98

In contrast, this same individual would be expected to respond to an item at about the 298 level with a probability of 36 percent. Although this person can be expected to demonstrate some success with tasks at the 300 level, performance would most likely be inconsistent — the individual would be expected to respond correctly less than half the time. Moreover, such an individual would have less than a 30 percent chance of responding correctly to tasks at around the 350 level on the prose scale.

The preceding paragraphs have focused on the probabilities of an individual with a particular (250) proficiency level successfully performing tasks along the prose scale. Now consider a task at the 253 level and the associated probabilities of responding correctly for individuals with varying levels of proficiencies. As shown in Table 2.1, the probability of responding correctly to this 253-level task for someone at the 150 level is only 13 percent. The probability increases to just over 40 percent for someone who is performing at the 200 level and, as expected, 78 percent for someone at the 250 level. The probability of responding correctly to this task increases to over 95 percent for individuals who score at or above the 300 level on the prose scale.

Interpretations of other tasks presented in Table 2.1 can be made in a similar manner; that is, the task at the 298 level is relatively difficult for individuals whose estimated proficiencies are between 150 and 200 on the scale. They have between a 1 and 7 percent chance of responding correctly to this or similar tasks. Individuals at the 300 level have an 82 percent chance of responding correctly, and individuals scoring at or above 350 would be expected to rarely miss this task or one like it.

To facilitate interpretation of proficiencies along each of the literacy scales, we have chosen to characterize them in terms of five levels. These levels reflect the extent to which one or more variables operate in ways that were initially conceptualized for the 1985 young adult literacy assessment and further amplified by Kirsch and Mosenthal[1] and the present DOL report. This work suggests that while literacy is not a single skill suited to all types of tasks, neither is it an infinite number of isolated skills each associated with a different type of material or purpose for reading. Rather there appears to be an ordered set of information-processing skills and strategies that may be called into play to accomplish the range of tasks falling along each of the scales. It is this ordering that we have attempted to capitalize on in describing the meaning of performance as it ranges from Level 1 through Level 5.

The remaining pages of this section characterize and profile literacy on each of the three scales. After a brief introduction, each scale is characterized in terms of the nature of the demands placed on the reader at each of the five levels. One or more exemplary tasks are described at each level. Performance is then profiled in terms of the average probability of people at selected proficiency levels estimated to be performing tasks correctly at each of the five levels and the percentages of selected DOL subpopulations demonstrating proficiency at each defined level. For comparison, percentages for similar subpopulations from the 1985 young adult literacy literacy assessment are also provided.

---

[1] I. S. Kirsch and P. B. Mosenthal. (1990). "Exploring document literacy: Variables underlying the performance of young adults," *Reading Research Quarterly*, 25, (1), 5-30.

● PROSE LITERACY

An important area of literacy is the knowledge and skills needed to understand and use information contained in various kinds of textual material. Prose materials used in this assessment are mostly expository — that is, they define or describe — since that constitutes much of the prose that adults read. These materials include texts from newspapers, magazines, brochures, and pamphlets. It is important to note that the texts used in this assessment are reprinted in their entirety and replicate the layout and typography of the original sources. As a result, the prose stimulus materials vary widely in length, density of information, and in the use of structural or organizational aids such as section or paragraph headings, italic or boldface type, and bullets.

The prose literacy scale contains 44 tasks that range from 164 to 465 on the scale. These tasks represent three major aspects of processing prose information: locating, integrating, and generating. *Locate* tasks require the reader to match information stated in a question or directive with information provided in the text. The match or relationship between the word(s) in the question and the text might be literal or synonymous or might require the reader to make an inference on the basis of one or more features. The *integrate* tasks in this assessment require the reader to pull together two or more pieces of information provided in the text. Such a task might require the reader to compare and contrast features given in the text with conditions provided in the question. In some cases, the information to be integrated is located within a single paragraph. In others, the reader must integrate information located in different paragraphs or sections of the text. The *generate* tasks in this assessment require readers to produce a written response where they not only have to process information in the text, but also to go beyond the text and draw on their background knowledge about a topic or make text-based inferences.

It is important to observe that tasks of each of these three types extend over a range of difficulty as a result of interaction with other variables that include:

- the number of categories or features of information in the question that the reader has to process;

- the number of categories or features of information in the text that can serve to distract the reader or that may seem plausible answers but are not correct;

- the degree to which information given in the question has less obvious identity with the information stated in the text; and,

- the length and density of the text.

Characterizing Proficiency Levels on the Prose Scale

The following discussion highlights some of the tasks on the prose scale and describes how their position on the scale seems to reflect various task characteristics mentioned above. Throughout the discussion, the numbers associated with specific tasks refer to the point on the scale at which the task is located based on an RP80 criterion. The headings for each level provide the percentage of the total JTPA, ES/UI, and young adult populations estimated to be performing at that level. The percentages of young adults from the 1985 assessment who were estimated to be performing at each level are shown here for comparison.

Prose Level 1 ≤ 225

JTPA	ES/UI	Young Adults
13.7%	12.2%	9.1%

Tasks falling at or below the 225 level (Level 1) on the prose scale require a reader to locate and match a single piece of requested information. Typically, the match between the question or directive and the text is literal, although sometimes a low-level inference may be necessary. In addition, the text is usually brief or has organizational aids such as paragraph headings or italics that help clue the appropriate places in the text to search for specific information. Finally, the key word or phrase appears only once in the text.

As an example, a passage reprinted in a newspaper about a marathon swimmer makes only one reference to food eaten during the swim. The directive asks the reader to "underline the sentence that tells what Ms. Chanin ate during the swim." This task at the 209 level requires matching "banana and honey sandwiches, hot chocolate, lots of water and granola bars" in the third paragraph with the word "ate" in the directive.

Individuals who score around 200 on the prose scale can be expected to perform these types of tasks successfully 80 percent of the time or better. Possibly because of their familiarity with the content, these readers will likely have some success with tasks at higher levels on the prose scale, but they would be expected to perform these

Swimmer completes Manhattan marathon

The Associated Press

NEW YORK—University of Maryland senior Stacy Chanin on Wednesday became the first person to swim three 28-mile laps around Manhattan.

Chanin, 23, of Virginia, climbed out of the East River at 96th Street at 9:30 p.m. She began the swim at noon on Tuesday.

A spokesman for the swimmer, Roy Brunett, said Chanin had kept up her strength with "banana and honey" sandwiches, hot chocolate, lots of water and granola bars."

Chanin has twice circled Man-hattan before and trained for the new feat by swimming about 28.4 miles a week. The Yonkers native has competed as a swimmer since she was 15 and hoped to persuade Olympic authorities to add a long-distance swimming event.

The Leukemia Society of America solicited pledges for each mile she swam.

In July 1983, Julie Ridge became the first person to swim around Manhattan twice. With her three laps, Chanin came up just short of Diana Nyad's distance record, set on a Florida-to-Cuba swim.

(Reduced from original copy.)

more difficult tasks with much less consistency — 50 percent of the time or less, depending on the task. (See Table 2.2 later in this section for references to probabilities of success at various levels on the prose scale.)

Prose Level 2 226-275

JTPA	ES/UI	Young Adults
26.2%	25.2%	23.1%

Tasks falling around the 250 level (from 226 to 275, or Level 2) on the scale place more varied demands on the reader. In contrast with Level 1 tasks where the key word or phrase to be matched appears only once in the text, the reader may need to discount distracting information that partially satisfies the question. With tasks in this range, the distracting information, if it appears, is widely separated from the sentence or paragraph containing the correct answer. For example, using the newspaper sports article reprinted above, one question at the 253 level directs the reader to identify the age at which Ms. Chanin began swimming competitively. In this instance, the swimmer's current age of 23 appears early in the text and serves as a plausible answer (distractor) for when she began competing, which is given later in the news story as age 15.

A	The clock does not run correctly on this clock radio. I tried fixing it, but I couldn't.	C	The alarm on my clock radio doesn't go off at the time I set. It rings 15-30 minutes later.
B	My clock radio is not working. It stopped working right after I used it for five days.	D	This radio is broken. Please repair and return by United Parcel Service to the address on my slip.

(Reduced from original copy.)

The majority of tasks around 250 continue to require the reader to locate information but frequently require matching more than a single piece of information. If more than a single-feature match is required, however, the needed information is found in adjoining text. The tasks also move from primarily literal matches to those involving synonyms or low text-based inferences. Moreover, tasks at this level begin to require the reader to integrate information, such as comparing and contrasting brief statements to judge which best represents a criterion. As shown above, the reader is asked to interpret a directive given in the form of an appliance warranty. This 273-level task requires that the reader identify the most appropriate of four statements describing the appliance's malfunction.

Although tasks requiring readers to generate information from text typically fall at higher levels on the prose scale, such tasks can be relatively easy. For example, a task at the 263 level requires the reader to generate a theme from a relatively short text (a poem) that uses a number of different metaphors to represent the single, relatively familiar concept of war. Despite the use of different metaphors, it is the repetition of the allusions to war that appears to make this task relatively easy.

Individuals who are estimated to be performing at the 250 level can be expected to perform these types of tasks successfully with around 80 percent probability. In turn, they can be expected to answer questions at or below the 225 level with better than 90 percent probability. For tasks above the 275 level, their probability of success falls to about 50 percent or less, depending on the task.

Prose Level 3 276-325

JTPA	ES/UI	Young Adults
38.5%	35.4%	39.4%

Tasks at about the 300 level (ranging from 276 to 325, Level 3) require the reader to search fairly dense text for information that is identified by making a literal or synonymous match on more than a single feature or to integrate two pieces of information from relatively long text that does not provide organizational aids. For example, a magazine article on parenting deals with the issue of physical punishment. A question at the 311 level directs the reader to "identify and list two reasons that Dr. Spock offers for not using physical punishment." While numerous statements throughout the article help satisfy the directive, much of the text deals with related concerns rather than direct summary statements. As a result, the reasons for not using physical punishment are embedded throughout the text and are not literally stated following a semantic cue such as "two good reasons for not using physical punishment are. . . ." In addition, distracting information is more closely tied to the words or phrases containing the necessary information for responding correctly.

Another task involving this text — at a somewhat lower level (283) — requires the reader to "list the two reasons given by the author why physical punishment is still widely accepted as a way to teach children right and wrong." In contrast to the task at the 311 level where the information is deeply embedded in the text without the advantage of semantic cues, this task can be answered by locating the place in the text that begins, "I think there are two reasons for this. The first is . . . . The second reason is . . . ."

The most difficult task (319) within this range requires the reader to synthesize the repetitive statements of an argument from a newspaper editorial in order to generate a theme or organizing principle. In this instance, the supporting statements are elaborated but widely separated in lengthy text.

Individuals who are estimated to score around 300 on the prose scale can be expected to perform these types of tasks successfully 80 percent of the time or better. The chance of responding correctly to tasks at or below the 225 level is high enough (about 98 percent) that they are likely to make few if any careless mistakes. Their chance of responding to tasks between the 226 and 275 levels is 90 percent or better. And, although respondents will likely have some success with tasks above the 325 level (i.e., at Levels 4 and 5) on the prose scale, they would be expected to perform these more complex tasks with less consistency — about 50 percent of the time or less, depending on the nature of the task.

Have You Ever Wanted To Strike Your Child?

Don't do it! Dr. Spock believes that physical discipline can cause lasting resentment in a sensitive child and may make a naughty child a real behavior problem.

Almost all parents with whom I've ever discussed the issue of physical punishment acknowledge that they've had a strong impulse to spank their children at one time or another, whether they believed in doing it or not: for instance, when a small child breaks a valuable object she has been told not to touch, or when a somewhat older child of six or seven runs into the street and a car just misses hitting him, or when an eleven-year-old is caught stealing and then brazenly tries to lie her way out of it. And it's the rare parent who has *never* given in to the impulse to slap or spank.

Parents tend to punish their children the same way their own parents punished them — whether it's by spanking or scolding or reasoning or withholding privileges. In this way patterns of discipline — both good and bad — are passed from one generation to the next.

Why is it that physical punishment, whether used occasionally or frequently, is still widely accepted as a way of teaching children what is right and what is wrong? I think there are two reasons for this. The first is the belief that it is simply the correct way of handling certain kinds of misbehavior, such as those I've mentioned earlier. The second reason is even more powerful, and it has to do with the parent's *reaction* to the misbehavior: the wave of anger that sweeps over the parent when a child misbehaves, *especially* when there is an element of defiance in an act or in an attitude. The child's challenge to the parent's authority causes a spasm of panic: If the parent doesn't act quickly and with force, the child might get the upper hand and, as a result, the parent might lose some control permanently. While I don't believe that a child should be able to get away with such deliberate misbehavior, I do believe there are other effective ways a parent can discipline his or her child without resorting to physical punishment.

You may wonder why I feel that other forms of discipline are preferable to physical punishment. What convinced me that spanking isn't necessary was that, in years of pediatric practice, I discovered there were many families in which the children were never spanked — and yet these children were cooperative, polite and kind. In some of these families the parents had not been physically punished in childhood, either. In others, the parents remembered the humiliation of being hit or spanked and were reacting to a conviction that the spankings they had received as children had had the wrong effect.

The reaction of the parents who don't spank their children because they themselves were spanked is worth considering because it raises the question of whether physical punishment does any harm. It is obvious that, when applied occasionally by loving parents, it can't do *much* harm — after all, millions of good men and women have been brought up in this way. But I think there are better ways of influencing children. When physical punishment is used frequently, especially by irritable or harsh parents, its unfavorable effects are noticeably multiplied. I believe physical punishment teaches children that might makes right and helps to turn some of them into bullies. Physical punishment leaves some sensitive children with a lasting resentment toward their parents for having humiliated them in this way. It encourages other children to feel that violence is not really bad and to think of physical force as a way of solving problems or settling disputes. As adults we know it is not an effective way of solving problems or settling disputes.

To me the most important reason for trying not to use physical punishment is that, if it is effective, it makes the child behave out of fear of the pain and out of fear of your anger. I think it's preferable for children to do the right thing because they love their parents and want to please them — not because they fear them. Then, as the children grow up, go to school, get jobs, marry and raise a family, they'll carry over this same attitude of getting along well in life by loving people, wanting to please them and cooperate with them — and receiving that love and cooperation in return.

What about other punishments parents can use, such as taking away a beloved toy for a day or so? To me, the loss of a privilege seems better than the indignity of being hit.

Isolating a child who is out of control has been used effectively in good day-care centers. Sending a child to his room for a given period of time works just as well at home, but isolation should be used in a calm, friendly spirit, as a way of helping the child to cool off.

To me, the best way of ensuring good behavior is for parents to show children love and respect — from infancy — and to set a good example. Then children look up to their parents and want to please them.

When parents shout and hit, they thwart a child's natural desire to please her parents, because the child's love and respect for them has been diminished. In the long run, that makes the parents' job of disciplining their children all the more difficult.

You may think your children would never respond to anything as mild as a good example or a polite request. If they have been used to rougher forms of discipline, I'll admit that they will seem insensitive at first to gentler methods. But they will gradually come around. I've seen the transformation take place in a day-care center, where a thick-skinned misbehaver began cooperating with a gentle teacher after he slowly learned that he could trust her to be kind to him.

One approach you could use to get the attention of a child who has learned to ignore anything but the most extreme forms of correction would be to go to her immediately when she misbehaves, put your arm around her and say quietly, "When you do that, it makes me unhappy. Please don't do it again!" If misbehavior is consistently corrected in this fashion, not only will the child learn that she can't persist in whatever it is that she's doing wrong, but, more importantly, she will come to enjoy a better relationship with you and the impulse to misbehave will diminish. Of course, it takes a good deal of patience for a parent to make the shift to this kind of gentle discipline. But the results are well worth the effort.

Although Dr. Spock cannot answer readers' letters individually, he will respond to them in his column. Please address your questions to Department DW, Redbook, 224 West 57th Street, New York, NY 10019.

Benjamin Spock: "Have You Ever Wanted to Strike Your Child?" Reprinted from *Redbook* by permission of the publisher.

(Reduced from original copy.)

BY JANE BRYANT QUINN

MONEY FACTS
7 New Rules for Financial Security

In the last few years almost everything about economics in this country has changed. Jobs are less secure. Incomes are flat. Air pockets develop, suddenly causing a city or an industry to drop. Even prosperous industries feel the breath of uncertainty, as the international economic order changes before our very eyes. Any way you look at it, you're facing a New Financial Dispensation —one with very different rules for financial security than we followed in the past:

1. Save more money. This rule may sound fruitless to a generation that grew up during a period when a penny saved was a penny lost. In the seventies the value of savings actually *declined* after taxes and inflation, but today savings accounts make money. They've become more essential, too, so everyone should try to save at least 10 percent of income. Most middle-class families can do it if they try.

2. Borrow less. It used to make sense to buy now and pay later because prices were likely to rise tomorrow. And loans were easy to pay off because incomes went up. Not anymore. Average incomes are not rising, and loans are often hard to pay off. The cost of borrowing is high — and most of the interest you pay is no longer tax deductible. Your financial security depends on changing that borrow-and-spend mind-set that worked in the past.

3. Buy a house only when you're putting down roots. Prices will not rise as much in the future as they did in the past. Housing values have even declined in many cities. To have a shot at getting your money back (after real estate commissions) you have to stay in the house four years or more.

This rule has two corollaries: *Don't buy a condominium if you can avoid it.* They usually don't rise in value as much as single-family homes and can be almost impossible to resell in a soft housing market. *If you've moved and can't sell your old house, don't just walk away from it.* The default will ruin your credit rating — and the bank may still try to collect. Instead, you may be able to negotiate a "deed in lieu of foreclosure" in which your house is handed over to the lender in return for an agreement not to sue you for any difference between what you owe and what the lender receives from the resale. This usually won't show up on your credit record.

4. Don't count on an inheritance to make up the retirement fund you failed to save. People are living longer, and frail old age is consuming their savings. The trend today is for children to get their "inheritance" earlier — in the form of college tuition or help with a down payment on their first home.

5. Push for a child-care benefit at work. It's the next essential employee benefit, and women haven't made enough of a fuss to get it. But now that some of the workers having babies are vice-presidents, some corporations are beginning to provide a wide range of child-care services: 1. information for locating baby-sitters; 2. payments to day-care centers to subsidize costs for employees' children; 3. day-care centers at the work site; 4. benefit plans that provide day-care payments to employees as a tax-free subsidy; 5. emergency-care centers, where a child can be left when an employee's regular day-care arrangements fail; 6. discounts at a national day-care chain.

Research this issue at your library and organize a study group. Talk to your firm's employee-benefits office. What you do can make a difference.

6. Keep close track of how well your employer is doing and whether your job is really necessary. Large layoffs continue as industry after industry hits the brick wall of competition, overexpansion or overindebtedness. If your company is in trouble, look immediately for another job; the first workers to leave find more opportunities than the last.

Now that pensions are vesting faster — often in only five years — you don't lose as much by changing jobs. You may be able to take a lump-sum pension disbursement with you when you leave. If you do, be sure to roll it over into an Individual Retirement Account. That will lower your taxes as well as protect your future.

In general, it pays to look for a new job in the same field so you can build on your experience. If your whole industry is slimming down, however, it's smarter to develop expertise in another area. You might have to take a pay cut on entering a new field, but the job could be more lasting in the long run. The rule: Stay flexible and always be willing to retrain if necessary.

7. Buy life and health insurance only from a company rated A-plus by A.M. Best for the past five to ten years. The insurance industry is not as strong as it used to be. Some 17.5 percent of the companies reporting to the National Association of Insurance Commissioners now appear on its "watch list" because of various financial weaknesses. In 39 states and Puerto Rico, guaranty funds pay some or all claims if your insurance company fails. But in the others (Alaska, Arkansas, California, District of Columbia, Louisiana, Missouri, New Jersey, Ohio, South Dakota, Tennessee, Wyoming) you'd have nowhere to go if your insurer failed. Several firms already have gone under, leaving their clients high and dry. With a long-time A-plus company, you ought to be all right.

(Reduced from original copy.)

Tasks at about the 350 level (326 to 375, Level 4) still require respondents to search for information, but at this level the search requires multiple-feature matching involving synonyms or low text-based inferences. An example of this type of task (332) involves reading a magazine article on rules for financial security. As detailed in the article, the reader is directed to list the types of child-care services that provide the employee with direct financial benefits. To respond correctly, the reader can use organizational aids in the text to locate the area dealing with the general topic. While locating the correct area of the text appears to be relatively easy, the difficulty of this task lies in determining what constitutes "direct" financial benefits.

The majority of the tasks in Level 4, however, require integrating across text — sometimes by comparing and contrasting numerous pieces of information to determine similarities. For example, a task at the 346 level directs the reader to identify and list two similarities between the new and old ways American Express handles charge-card receipts.

■

American Express' Way of Handling the Flood of Charge Card Receipts

How the new way stacks up against the old way

The New Way:
1 Image processing camera converts receipts to electronic digital image and paper receipts are discarded. 2 Digital image is scanned for account and invoice numbers by optical character (99% accuracy). In the future, computers will also read handwritten charge amounts. 3 Charge amounts are entered by computer operator from image displayed on computer screen. 4 Images are sorted electronically. 5 Bills, with images of receipts, are printed by laser and mailed to cardholders. 6 Images of receipts are stored permanently on optical discs.

The Old Way:
1 Paper receipts are microfilmed for 2 permanent storage, then 3 scanned for account and invoice number by optical character reader (82% accuracy). 4 Charge amounts are entered by computer operator from receipts. 5 A code containing all the information is printed on the receipts. 6 Paper receipts are sorted. 7 Bills are generated by mainframe computer. 8 Receipts and bills are joined and mailed.

■

Individuals who are estimated to score around 350 on this scale can be expected to perform successfully the types of tasks shown here, as well as others like them, 80 percent of the time or better. These same individuals can be expected to successfully perform all of the preceding tasks on this scale with better than a 90 percent probability. This means that individuals demonstrating 350-level proficiency would be expected to respond correctly to at least nine out of 10 tasks falling between the 150 and 325 levels. Moreover, although respondents will likely have some success with tasks above the 375 level on the prose scale, they would be expected to perform these more complex tasks with less consistency.

Prose Level 5 ≥ 376

JTPA	ES/UI	Young Adults
4.6%	5.0%	4.7%

A task (RP80 of 364) bordering on the next level ranging upward from 376 (Level 5) requires the reader to generate a theme from very brief text using a single unfamiliar metaphor (a poem). It appears that this task is difficult because it includes an unfamiliar metaphor with no repetition of the theme to assist the reader in interpretation.

∎

> The pedigree of honey
> Does not concern the Bee —
> A clover, any time, to him
> Is Aristocracy —   (Emily Dickinson)

∎

Other tasks that reach or surpass 375 require the reader to search for information in dense text containing numerous plausible distractors, to make broad text-based inferences, and to compare and contrast numerous pieces of complex information to identify differences. Among these tasks is one using the passage shown earlier describing new and old ways of handling charge-card receipts. The task at this level requires the reader to contrast two differences between the new and old ways of processing these receipts.

Individuals at this highest level on the scale can be expected to perform successfully virtually all tasks contained in this assessment. They have demonstrated proficiency in locating, integrating, and generating information using a wide range of printed materials.

Profiling Proficiencies on the Prose Scale

Table 2.2 summarizes data provided about each of the five proficiency levels defined along the prose scale. Starting at the left side of the table, the first column defines the range of each level on a 500-point scale, the second column provides a brief description of the processing demands associated with each level, and the third column contains the average RP80 value across the tasks located within a particular level, followed by columns displaying the average probability of getting these tasks correct at selected levels of proficiency. To understand how to interpret this information, it will be useful to look at an example that focuses on a particular proficiency level and the associated probabilities of responding correctly for individuals with different levels of proficiency. The third column shows that the average RP80 value of tasks falling within Level 2 (between 226 and 275 on the prose scale) is 256. The figures to the right of this column show that someone with an estimated proficiency level of 200 is expected to answer the average Level 2 task correctly with a probability of 39 percent — that is, only about four out of 10 times. In contrast, someone estimated to have a proficiency of 250 would be expected to answer these types of tasks correctly 76 percent of the time while someone with a proficiency of 300 would be expected, on average, to have a better than 90 percent chance of responding correctly to Level 2 tasks. Now consider the probability of an individual with a proficiency level of 250 successfully performing tasks at each of the five levels. Figures in the column headed 250 indicate that such a person has a 94 percent chance of responding correctly to Level 1 tasks. This probability drops to 76 percent for Level 2 tasks, 47 percent for Level 3 tasks, and below 30 percent for tasks at Levels 4 and 5 on the prose scale.

The data displayed on the right side of Table 2.2 depict the percentages of JTPA and ES/UI populations estimated to be performing within each of the five levels on the prose literacy scale. For comparison, similar information is also presented from the 1985 assessment of young adults. These percentages are presented for the total populations as well as for race/ethnicity and level of education.

Total Populations

As shown in Table 2.2, there are no marked differences in the distributions of proficiencies among the total DOL populations. For example, about 13 percent from

Table 2.2	Prose Literacy*								

Levels	Description of Prose Tasks at Each of Five Levels	Average RP 80 at Each Level	Average Probability at Selected Proficiency Levels					TOTAL	
			200	250	300	350	400		
Level 1 0-225	Prose tasks at this level are the least demanding in terms of what the reader must do to produce a correct response. Typically, tasks at this level require the reader to locate one piece of information in which there is a literal match between the question and the stimulus material. If a distractor or plausible right answer is present, it tends to be located away from where the correct information is found.	192	81	94	98	100	100	JTPA ES/UI Young Adults	13.7 (1.7) 12.2 (2.4) 9.1 (0.8)
Level 2 226-275	Some of the prose tasks of this level still require the reader to locate on a single feature of information; however, these tasks tend to occur in materials where there are several distractors or where the match is based on low-level inferences. Tasks at this level also begin to require the reader to integrate information by pulling together two or more pieces or by comparing and contrasting information.	256	39	76	94	99	100	JTPA ES/UI Young Adults	26.2 (1.7) 25.2 (1.3) 23.1 (0.8)
Level 3 276-325	Tasks at this level tend to require the reader to search fairly dense text for literal or synonymous matches on the basis of more than one feature of information or to integrate information from relatively long text that does not contain organizational aids such as headings.	298	17	47	81	95	99	JTPA ES/UI Young Adults	38.5 (2.1) 35.4 (1.3) 39.4 (1.3)
Level 4 326-375	Tasks at this level continue to demand more from the reader. Not only are multiple-feature matching and integration of information from complex displays maintained, the degree of inferencing required by the reader is increased. Conditional information is frequently present in tasks at this level that must be taken into account.	349	13	29	56	81	93	JTPA ES/UI Young Adults	17.0 (0.9) 22.3 (1.6) 23.8 (1.1)
Level 5 376-500	At this level tasks typically require the reader to search for information in dense text containing plausible distractors, to make high text-based inferences or use specialized background knowledge as well as compare and contrast sometimes complex information.	417	14	24	38	56	73	JTPA ES/UI Young Adults	4.6 (0.7) 5.0 (0.6) 4.7 (0.8)

*The numbers in parentheses are estimated standard errors.

	RACE/ETHNICITY			EDUCATION				
White	Black	Hispanic		0-8	9-12 No Dip.	H.S. Dip. or GED	Some Postsec.	College Degree
9.7 (1.2)	20.9 (4.0)	27.6 (4.6)		49.2 (5.0)	22.6 (2.1)	8.5 (1.2)	3.7 (1.4)	2.3 (2.2)
3.7 (0.5)	18.9 (4.7)	33.3 (5.6)		64.5 (9.6)	30.9 (7.8)	9.6 (1.1)	5.3 (1.3)	3.3 (1.5)
5.3 (0.9)	28.7 (2.0)	16.0 (1.9)		64.9(10.0)	33.0 (3.6)	10.1 (1.3)	2.5 (0.6)	0.1 (0.1)
23.6 (1.9)	36.6 (3.0)	24.5 (5.5)		25.9 (3.8)	43.9 (3.1)	20.8 (2.2)	18.5 (2.7)	4.8 (2.0)
18.5 (1.5)	43.9 (2.3)	32.5 (6.0)		30.0 (8.5)	37.4 (7.1)	28.6 (2.0)	22.3 (2.8)	12.4 (1.8)
19.2 (1.1)	41.6 (2.5)	32.5 (3.3)		32.6(10.3)	42.7 (3.6)	31.4 (1.8)	17.9 (1.6)	5.1 (1.1)
41.1 (2.2)	30.4 (3.7)	39.4 (5.5)		21.4 (4.3)	26.9 (2.3)	47.9 (3.0)	42.6 (2.7)	28.7(10.3)
40.1 (1.4)	29.0 (2.9)	25.5 (2.9)		5.2 (3.6)	24.7 (3.9)	41.6 (2.2)	38.6 (2.8)	32.7 (2.3)
41.9 (1.4)	24.5 (2.2)	36.3 (3.8)		2.5 (1.9)	22.2 (3.5)	43.6 (1.8)	42.0 (2.4)	39.8 (2.7)
19.9 (1.5)	11.3 (1.5)	6.2 (2.2)		3.5 (2.3)	5.8 (1.9)	18.4 (1.0)	28.7 (3.8)	39.9 (7.5)
29.9 (1.1)	8.0 (1.1)	8.6 (1.8)		0.3 (0.3)	6.8 (1.1)	18.4 (1.4)	29.3 (2.4)	35.3 (2.2)
27.9 (1.2)	4.7 (1.0)	14.7 (3.5)		0.0 (0.0)	2.1 (0.9)	14.0 (1.4)	31.4 (2.3)	42.7 (3.1)
5.7 (1.1)	0.9 (0.4)	2.3 (2.3)		0.0 (0.0)	0.8 (0.6)	4.4 (1.5)	6.4 (1.6)	24.3 (6.7)
7.9 (0.8)	0.2 (0.2)	0.0 (0.0)		0.0 (0.0)	0.2 (0.1)	1.8 (0.4)	4.5 (0.9)	16.3 (2.3)
5.7 (0.9)	0.6 (0.3)	0.5 (0.4)		0.0 (0.0)	0.1 (0.1)	0.8 (0.3)	6.1 (1.3)	12.3 (2.1)

each DOL group are estimated to be performing the range of Level 1 tasks (at or below the 225 level). In comparison with young adults, a significantly larger percentage of JTPA applicants demonstrate proficiency at this level — 13.7 compared with 9.1. Since these individuals demonstrate proficiency only with prose tasks requiring literal, one-feature matches in short, relatively uncomplicated texts, it would seem that their literacy skills would place the most severe restrictions on full participation in our increasingly complex society. They are estimated to perform consistently only about four tasks or 10 percent of the exercises represented on the prose scale. Tasks at this level have an average RP80 of 192. Moreover, as shown in Section 3 of this report, they are performing at about the level of those DOL respondents who report not attaining more than an eighth-grade education.

Roughly one-fourth of the applicants in each of these three populations is estimated to score in the Level 2 range (226 to 275) on the prose scale. At this level, individuals can be expected to demonstrate more complex skills involving integration and generation of information and to succeed consistently on about one-third of the prose tasks in this assessment. Their specific skills are limited to using short, uncomplicated texts or texts containing numerous repetitions of an argument. Demonstrated proficiency in this range still probably limits their full participation in society. The average difficulty of tasks at this level is 256. Again, as indicated in Section 3 of this report, these individuals are, on average, reading at about the level of those who report dropping out of school before earning a high school diploma.

As shown in Table 2.2, some 35 to 40 percent of the DOL and young adult populations demonstrate performance in the Level 3 range (276 to 325). The only significant difference at this level is that a smaller percentage of ES/UI participants perform at this level than 21- to 25-year-olds. Individuals performing at Level 3 demonstrate consistent success in dealing with literal or synonymous matching of information on more than a single feature and with the integration of two pieces of information from fairly lengthy, dense texts that do not provide organizational or structural cues. These individuals can be expected to perform successfully on 70 percent of the prose tasks contained in this assessment. These tasks have an average RP80 value of 298. Although there is room for improvement, it is likely that these individuals are not encountering major difficulty in using the printed texts they encounter most frequently in their work and everyday lives. In fact, these individuals are performing at about the level of JTPA and ES/UI program participants who report earning a high school diploma or GED.

Some 25 percent of the DOL populations demonstrate skills at or above Level 4 (326 and above). A significantly smaller percentage of JTPA applicants perform at

Level 4 compared with both ES/UI participants and young adults. While only about 5 percent of each population attain Level 5, as a group these individuals are succeeding on 90 percent or more of the tasks contained on the prose scale. These tasks require the reader to locate and integrate information from complex texts. The most challenging of these tasks require the reader to make broad text-based inferences or use specialized background knowledge. These skills are commensurate with the skills of individuals who report a two-year college degree or higher. The 20 to 30 percent of the DOL populations who demonstrate proficiencies at or above Level 4 appear to represent an untapped resource.

Race/Ethnicity

A significantly higher percentage of White and Hispanic JTPA applicants attain Level 1 scores than White and Hispanic young adults — 9.7 and 27.6 as compared with 5.3 and 16.0, respectively. At the same time, a significantly smaller percentage of White and Hispanic JTPA applicants obtain scores in the Level 4 range than do White and Hispanic young adults — 19.9 and 6.2 compared with 27.9 and 14.7, respectively.

In contrast, the reverse pattern of results is shown for Black JTPA applicants as compared with Black young adults. Here we see a smaller (though not quite significant) percentage of Black JTPA applicants represented at Level 1 as compared with Black young adults (20.9 versus 28.7, respectively), while a significantly larger percentage of Black JTPA applicants than Black young adults perform at Level 4 — 11.3 compared with 4.7, respectively.

The trend for Black ES/UI participants when compared with Black young adults is similar to the pattern noted for JTPA eligible Black applicants. That is, a smaller percentage of Black ES/UI participants attain Level 1 scores (18.9 as compared with 28.7, respectively), while a larger percentage attain Level 4 scores (8.0 versus 4.7, respectively). In contrast, among Hispanic ES/UI participants, a larger percentage attain Level 1 (33.3 as compared with 16.0, respectively), while a smaller percentage demonstrate proficiency at Level 4 (8.6 versus 14.7, respectively). It should be noted, however, that the difference in percentage at Level 1 does not reach statistical significance for Black participants nor does the difference for Hispanic applicants at Level 4. There are no significant differences between the ES/UI White program participants and the subgroup of White young adults.

These patterns notwithstanding[2], Black and Hispanic populations are disproportionately represented at the low and high prose proficiency levels when

[2]See Table 6.3, p. 131, in I. S. Kirsch and A. Jungeblut. (1992). *Profiling the literacy proficiencies of JTPA and ES/UI populations: Final report to the Department of Labor.* (Princeton, NJ: Educational Testing Service.)

compared with White populations. Given that the comparisons at Levels 1, 2, 3, and 4 are significant, it is noteworthy that some 50 to 70 percent of Black and Hispanic respondents perform at Levels 1 or 2 compared with about 20 to 35 percent of White respondents. Conversely, while 8 to 15 percent of Black and Hispanic populations demonstrate proficiency at Levels 4 and 5 on the prose scale, some 25 to 40 percent of White respondents attain these highest levels.

Levels of Education

The distributions of educational attainment are notably similar for the ES/UI and young adult populations. However, a larger percentage of JTPA eligible applicants report lower levels of attainment than is the case for either ES/UI participants or young adults. Thus, a substantially smaller percentage of JTPA applicants report some postsecondary experience or a college degree than either ES/UI participants or young adults.

Not surprisingly, the general pattern of results for the three populations is that educational attainment is positively related to demonstrated literacy proficiency. That is, across the three populations, a greater proportion of individuals who report lower levels of educational attainment are found in the lower levels on the prose scale. For example, the highest proportion of individuals scoring within Level 1 are those reporting zero to eight years of education — 65 percent of young adults, 49 percent of JTPA applicants, and 65 percent of ES/UI participants. Conversely, the highest proportion of individuals demonstrating proficiency at Level 5 report attaining a college degree — 12 percent of young adults, 24 percent of JTPA applicants, and 16 percent of ES/UI participants. Of particular concern is the fact that a substantial percentage of individuals who report earning a high school diploma or GED demonstrate very limited skills. That is, some 30 to 40 percent of JTPA and ES/UI participants as well as young adults from the earlier study who report this level of education are estimated to have literacy skills limited to Levels 1 and 2.

Perhaps the most interesting findings relating to educational attainment are those shown in Table 2.2 for JTPA eligible applicants. Despite the fact that JTPA applicants report, on average, lower levels of educational attainment than do young adults, larger percentages of these JTPA applicants demonstrate proficiencies at Levels 3 and 4 than do young adults with similar levels of education. For example, 21 and 4 percent of JTPA applicants reporting zero to eight years of education are found to reach Levels 3 and 4 on the prose scale, respectively, as compared with 3 and 0 percent of young adults. Moreover, virtually no young adult reporting a college degree performs at Level 1 while 2 percent of JTPA applicants reporting a college degree perform at this level. The only significant differences for ES/UI participants that parallel the trend noted between young adults and JTPA applicants are found among college graduates scoring at Levels 1 and 2 — the percentages are 3.3 and 12.4, respectively, for ES/UI participants and 0.1 and 5.1 for young adults.

● DOCUMENT LITERACY

One important aspect of being literate in a technologically advancing society is possessing the knowledge and skills needed to process information found in documents.[3] Document literacy tasks require readers to locate and use information contained in materials such as tables, schedules, charts, graphs, maps, and forms. Skills needed to process these materials seem to involve strategies associated with locating information in complex arrays. Successful performance may be contingent upon procedural knowledge associated with transferring and entering information given in one source or document to another, such as the knowledge required to complete an application or an order form. Such tasks are not only important in our personal lives, but for many individuals, these tasks are also a necessary part of managing a household and meeting job requirements. In fact, research has shown that adults spend more time reading documents than any other type of material.[4]

The document literacy scale used in this assessment contains some 93 tasks that range from 90 to 470 on the scale. Questions and directives associated with these tasks are basically of three types: locating, cycling, and integrating. *Locating* tasks require readers to match one or more features of information stated in the question to either identical or synonymous information given in the document. *Cycling* tasks, although requiring the reader to locate and match one or more features, differ in that they require the reader to engage in a series of feature matches to satisfy the conditions given in the question. The *integrating* tasks typically require the reader to compare and contrast information in adjacent parts of the document.

As with the prose tasks, tasks of each type of question or directive extend over a range of difficulty as a result of interactions among several variables or task characteristics that include:

---

[3] I. S. Kirsch and P. B. Mosenthal. (1990). "Exploring document literacy: Variables underlying the performance of young adults," *Reading Research Quarterly*, 25, (1), 5-30.

[4] J. T. Guthrie, M. Seifert, and I. S. Kirsch. (1986). "Effects of education, occupation, and setting on reading practices," *American Educational Research Journal*, 23, 151-160.

- the number of categories or features of information in the question that the reader has to process;

- the number of categories or features of information in the text that can serve to distract the reader or that may seem plausible but are not correct;

- the degree to which the information asked for in the question has less obvious identity with the information stated in the document; and,

- the structure of the document.

Characterizing Proficiency Levels on the Document Scale

The following discussion highlights some of the tasks along the document scale and describes how their relative positions along the scale seem to reflect various combinations of the variables mentioned above. Throughout the discussion, the numbers associated with specific tasks refer to their location on the scale, based on an RP80 criterion. The heading separating each level provides the percentages of the total JTPA and ES/UI populations estimated to be performing at this level. The percentages of young adults from the 1985 assessment who are estimated to be performing at each level are shown here for comparison.

Document Level ■1■ ≤ 225

JTPA	ES/UI	Young Adults
14.1%	13.1%	8.0%

Tasks falling at or below the 225 level (within the Level 1 range) on this scale typically require the reader to make a one-feature, literal match between information stated in the question and information provided in the document. In some instances, the question or directive asks for personal background information that must be entered into an appropriate location on the document. For example, the simplest task on this scale (RP80 of 90) directs the reader to "Look at the Social Security card. Sign your name on the line marked signature." Several characteristics combine to make this task easy. First, it may be assumed that the information requested (one's own name) is known. Second, there is only one category or feature of information that must be provided. Third, there is only one place on the document where the reader may respond.

Tasks within this level that are more difficult than signing the Social Security card require matching a single piece of information or feature from the question or directive with information in the body of the document. Several tasks that were developed around a form used in setting up a meeting require the reader to locate specific information, as opposed to entering known, personal background information. For example, the reader must supply information that is given on the form regarding the time and date of a meeting — RP80 values of 180 and 183, respectively. These two tasks each require the reader to match a single, literal feature from the form that contains no distracting information — i.e., only a single reference is made in the document to date or time.

THEATER TRIP

A charter bus will leave from the bus stop (near the Conference Center) at 4 p.m., giving you plenty of time for dinner in New York. Return trip will start from West 45th Street directly following the plays. Both theaters are on West 45th Street. Allow about 1 1/2 hours for the return trip.

Time: 4 p.m., Saturday, November 20
Price: "On the Town"   Ticket and bus $11
        "Sleuth"   Ticket and bus $8.50
Limit: Two tickets per person

Document tasks in this range become more difficult as the task characteristics described above combine with one another. For instance, tasks at this level require the reader to match a single, literal feature in documents that contain one or two distractors or plausible answers. A task at the 198 level, for example, directs the reader to circle the cost for a ticket and bus trip to see "On the Town." Although the reader simply locates the line labeled "price" and circles the dollar amount associated with "On the Town," the cost given in the document for "Sleuth" can serve as a distractor.

Another instance of the ways in which task characteristics combine to increase task difficulty involves the completion of a section of a job application form. As with signing the Social Security card, the task is to provide single pieces of personal information. This time, however, to satisfy the directive, the respondent must provide several pieces of information through a series or cycle of one-feature matches. As a result of the need to cycle through the document several times, this particular task is found at the 218 level.

■

1. You have gone to an employment center for help in finding a job. You know that this center handles many different kinds of jobs. Also, several of your friends who have applied here have found jobs that appeal to you.

    The agent has taken your name and address and given you the rest of the form to fill out. Complete the form so the employment center can help you get a job.

    Birth date_____ Age____ Sex: Male____ Female____

    Height_____ Weight_____ Health_____

    Last grade completed in school_____

    Kind of work wanted:

        Part-time_____   Summer_____

        Full-time_____   Year-round_____

(Reduced from original copy.)

■

Another cycle task falling at about this same level (RP80 of 205) directs the reader to look over a list of food to buy and then, using an advertisement from a supermarket, circle four things on the list for which there are savings coupons. Again, to respond correctly, the reader makes four, one-feature matches between the shopping list and the printed set of coupons.

Individuals who perform in this range on the scale demonstrate proficiency at entering personal background information onto clearly identified or structured forms and locating single pieces of information with or without distractor information present. Individuals performing around the 200 level can be expected to perform these types of tasks successfully across a broad range of rather uncomplicated documents with a high degree of consistency — that is, about 80 percent of the time. While they can also demonstrate skill at using other documents involving tasks requiring more complex processing of information, their chances for success on these tasks drop to about 50 percent or less, depending on the task. (See Table 2.3 for references to probabilities of success at various levels on the document scale.)

Document Level 2 226-275

JTPA	ES/UI	Young Adults
37.3%	30.1%	24.2%

Tasks at the next range of complexity (226 to 275, or Level 2) on the scale still require the reader to match on a single feature; however, several distractors may be present or the match (rather than being literal) may be based on synonyms or text-based inferences. One such task at the 234 level directs the reader to look at a pediatric dosage chart and underline the sentence that indicates how often the medication may be administered. To respond successfully, the reader needs to associate the word "administered" in the directive to the word "given" in the document by looking at information outside the table itself.

Recommend

Tempra
ALCOHOL-FREE ASPIRIN-FREE
ACETAMINOPHEN

A Caring Sponsor of
Ronald McDonald House
Ronald McDonald House is a program of Ronald McDonald Children's Charities®

Pediatric Dosage Chart   Drops, Syrup, & Chewables

Age	Approximate Weight Range*	Drops	Syrup	Chewables 80 mg	Chewables 160 mg
† Under 3 mo	Under 13 lb	½ dropper	¼ tsp	—	—
† 3 to 9 mo	13-20 lb	1 dropper	½ tsp	—	—
† 10 to 24 mo	21-26 lb	1 ½ droppers	¾ tsp	—	—
2 to 3 yr	27-35 lb	2 droppers	1 tsp	2 tablets	—
4 to 5 yr	36-43 lb	3 droppers	1 ½ tsp	3 tablets	1 ½ tablets
6 to 8 yr	44-62 lb	—	2 tsp	4 tablets	2 tablets
9 to 10 yr	63-79 lb	—	2 ½ tsp	5 tablets	2 ½ tablets
11 yr	80-89 lb	—	3 tsp	6 tablets	3 tablets
12 yr and older	90 lb & over	—	3-4 tsp	6-8 tablets	3-4 tablets

† Consult with physician before administering to children under the age of 2 years.
Dosage may be given every 4 hours as needed but not more than 5 times daily.
How Supplied:
Drops: Each 0.8 ml dropper contains 80 mg (1.23 grains) acetaminophen.
Syrup: Each 5 ml teaspoon contains 160 mg (2.46 grains) acetaminophen.
Chewables: Regular tablets contain 80 mg (1.23 grains) acetaminophen each. Double strength tablets contain 160 mg (2.46 grains) acetaminophen each.
* If child is significantly under- or overweight, dosage may need to be adjusted accordingly.
The weight categories in this chart are designed to approximate effective dose ranges of 10-15 milligrams per kilogram.
(Current Pediatric Diagnosis and Treatment. 8th ed. CH Kempe and HK Silver, ed. Lange Medical Publications: 1984, p. 1079.)
LA-1451-2-88 © 1988, Bristol-Myers U.S. Pharmaceutical and Nutritional Group • Evansville, Indiana 47721 U.S.A.

(c) 1988, Bristol-Myers Pharmaceutical and Nutritional Group.

(Reduced from original copy.)

Other tasks falling in the Level 2 range (from 226 to 275) on the document scale require the reader to either match on the basis of two categories of information with distractors present, or compare information on a similar feature across different but adjacent parts of a document. In the first instance, a task at the 261 level directs the reader to look at a pay stub summarizing wage information. The reader is asked to write the "gross pay for this year to date."

HOURS				PERIOD ENDING 03/15/85		REGULAR	OVERTIME	GROSS	DEF ANN	NET PAY
REGULAR	2ND SHIFT	OVERTIME	TOTAL		CURRENT	62500		62500		45988
500			500		YEAR TO DATE			426885		

TAX DEDUCTIONS					OTHER DEDUCTIONS					
	FED W H	STATE W H	CITY W/H	FICA	CR UNION		UNITED FD	PERS INS	MISC	MISC CODE
CURRENT	10894	1375		3831						
YEAR TO DATE	73498	8250		26167						

NON-NEGOTIABLE

OTHER DEDUCTIONS					
CODE	TYPE	AMOUNT	CODE	TYPE	AMOUNT
07	DEN	412			

(Reduced from original copy.)

If the reader fails to match on both categories — gross pay and year to date — he or she is likely to provide an incorrect amount, such as $625.00 if the match search is on the category "gross," or $261.67 if the match involves only the category "year to date." The other type of task — where the reader needs to compare information — is demonstrated by a line graph depicting the purchasing power of the minimum wage in current and constant dollars.

The question asks the reader to determine, based on constant 1975 dollars, the year in which the minimum wage exceeded $2.20 an hour. To respond correctly to this task at the 260 level, the reader either needs to look along the line representing $2.20 and then check down the column for 1978, the only year in which the line for constant dollars exceeds $2.20, or to identify the line representing constant 1975 dollars and then compare the various points to determine where the line exceeds $2.20. A similar kind of task, also at this level (RP80 of 268), directs the reader to

PURCHASING POWER OF MINIMUM WAGE

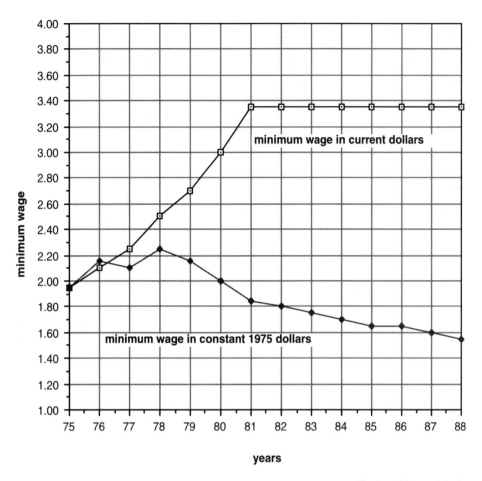

minimum wage in current dollars

minimum wage in constant 1975 dollars

years

(Reduced from original copy.)

look at another line graph showing a company's seasonal sales over a three-year period. The question asks the reader to predict the level of sales for the spring of the following year based on the graph's pattern. (See page 38).

Individuals who are estimated to be in the score range of Level 2 on the document scale can perform the types of locate and integrate tasks described and shown here about 80 percent of the time. Their proficiency at performing tasks up to the 225 level exceeds 90 percent. Again, such individuals will demonstrate some successes with tasks at higher levels on the scale — above the 275 level — but will do so, on average, around half the time or less, depending on the tasks.

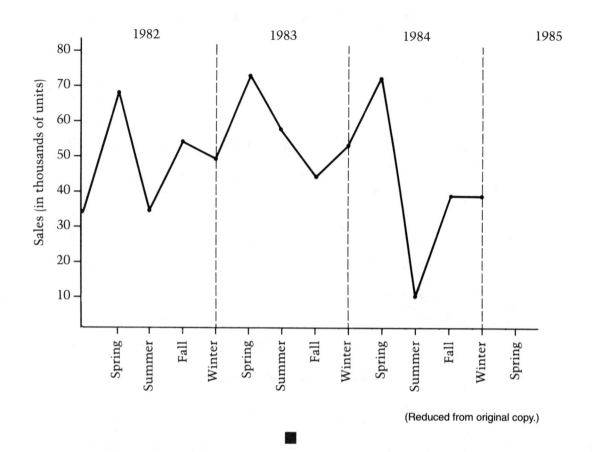

(Reduced from original copy.)

Document Level **3** **276-325**
JTPA **ES/UI** **Young Adults**
35.4% 35.9% 39.7%

Tasks falling around the 300 level (between 276 and 325, or Level 3) continue to require the reader to locate and integrate information. Tasks at this level, however, tend to involve the matching of more than two features of information in more complex displays of information. In these complex displays, distractors are typically present within the same row or column as the correct answer. One task at the 306 level directs the reader to use a table containing nested information to determine the type of sandpaper to buy if one needs "to smooth wood in preparation for sealing and plans to buy garnet sandpaper." This task requires matching not only on more than a single feature of information but also on features that are not always superordinate categories. For example, "preparation for sealing" is subordinated or nested under the category "wood," while the type of sandpaper is under the main category or heading of "garnet." In addition, there are three other types of sandpaper that the reader might select that partially satisfy the question.

■

ABRASIVE SELECTION GUIDE																	
MATERIAL & OPERATION	**PRODUCTION®**					**GARNET**				**WETORDRY®**				**FRE-CUT®**		**EMERY**		
	EC	C	M	F	EF	C	M	F	EF	VF	EF	SF	UF	VF	EF	C	M	F
WOOD																		
Paint Removal	■	■																
Heavy Stock Removal						■												
Moderate Stock Removal			■															
Preparation for Sealing				■	■													
After Sealer								■				■						
Between Coats												■			■			
After Final Coat																		
METAL																		
Rust and Paint Removal	■	■														■		
Light Stock Removal			■														■	
Preparation for Priming																		■
Finishing and Polishing						■					■	■						
After Primer											■	■						
Between Coats												■						
After Final Coat													■					
PLASTIC & FIBERGLASS																		
Shaping		■	■															
Light Stock Removal				■		■												
Finishing & Scuffing										■			■					

EC = Extra Coarse   C = Coarse   M = Medium   F = Fine   VF = Very Fine   EF = Extra Fine   SF = Super Fine   UF = Ultra Fine

SAFETY INFORMATION: ■ Use particle/dust mask or other means to prevent inhalation of sanding dust.   ■ When using power tools, follow manufacturer's recommended procedures and safety instructions.
■ Wear approved safety goggles when sanding.

Reprint by permission of and copyrighted by the 3M Co.

(Reduced from original copy.)

■

A similar type of task falling in Level 3 (RP80 of 309) requires the reader to select one of two tables showing the value of bonds based on monthly savings rate, age, and interest level. The task directs the respondents to identify how much money they would need to save each month for investment in 10 percent bonds to ensure that by age 18 their newborn child would have at least $55,000 to cover estimated education costs.

Individuals who are estimated to be in Level 3 on the document scale demonstrate proficiency at doing these more complex tasks with a high degree of consistency — around 80 percent. In addition, they can be expected to perform some of the less complex tasks more than 90 percent of the time and the least complex tasks (at or below 225) with few, if any, careless mistakes. As noted before, they will also demonstrate some success with higher-level tasks, although their consistency in performing these tasks will not, on average, exceed 50 percent.

HIGH INTEREST
U.S.
Savings Bonds

HOW DOLLARS FOR EDUCATION CAN GROW:

...at 7.5% (guaranteed minimum)

Child's Age Now	Value of Bonds at Age 18 through Monthly Savings of $25	$50	$100
Birth	$11,092.22	$22,184.44	$44,368.88
6	5,682.14	11,364.28	22,728.56
12	2,203.94	4,407.88	8,815.76

...at 10% (sample market-based rate)

Child's Age Now	Value of Bonds at Age 18 through Monthly savings of $25	$50	$100
Birth	$14,358.32	$28,716.64	$57,433.28
6	6,593.28	13,186.56	26,373.12
12	2,269.10	4,538.20	9,076.40

If you begin saving just $25 a month at your child's birth, and the market-based rate averages 10% over the life of your Bonds, your child will have $14,358.32 at age 18 — just in time for college!

BUILD YOUR RETIREMENT SAVINGS:

You'll benefit from two options:
1. You can cash Bonds to supplement your retirement income, reporting the tax-deferred interest as income on your Federal taxes. You'll probably be in a lower tax bracket — and if you're over 65, your double exemption means even more money to enjoy.
2. Or you can continue deferring Federal taxes by exchanging your Series EE Bonds, Series E Bonds, and Savings Notes for Series HH Bonds, which pay you interest semiannually by Treasury checks. You don't have to pay tax on the accumulated interest on your exchanged Bonds until the HH Bonds are cashed or reach final maturity. This way, you keep your principal intact, have a steady income for 10 years, and — when the HH Bonds are cashed — the tax will be levied at your lower post-retirement rate.

NOTE: Series EE Bonds, Savings Notes, and most Series E Bonds will receive market-based rates (or their current guarantees, if higher) when held until November 1, 1987 or longer. Series E Bonds that reach their 40th anniversary before then will receive their present guaranteed yield to final maturity, but aren't eligible for the market-based rates. Bonds issued before April 1952 stop earning interest exactly 40 years after their issue date and should be converted to HH Bonds or redeemed.

Biweekly Savings	At 5 Years 7.5%	At 10 Years 7.5%	10%
$ 3.75	$ 573.27	$ 1,408.17	$ 1,570.49
6.25	957.55	2,356.91	2,633.95
12.50	1,920.00	4,727.96	5,286.86
25.00	3,846.04	9,469.92	10,597.26
50.00	7,692.08	18,939.84	21,194.52
100.00	15,384.16	27,879.68	42,389.04

Monthly Savings	At 5 Years 7.5%	At 10 Years 7.5%	10%
$ 6.25	$ 434.70	$ 1,074.00	$ 1,196.90
12.50	874.52	2,161.04	2,411.42
25.00	1,759.34	4,348.46	4,863.34
50.00	3,518.68	8,696.92	9,726.68
100.00	7,037.36	17,393.84	19,453.36

The longer you hold your Bonds, the faster your money grows. Join your Payroll Savings Plan today — and watch *your* savings grow!

U.S. Savings Bonds

(Reduced from original copy.)

EL PASO GAS & ELECTRIC

Account number:
0320 1234 567 891 0

PAMELA B. MORGAN
3120 CROSS ST.
EL PASO, TX 79924

Next meter reading:
Wednesday, Sep. 7, 88

8382

Electric Service

This meter reading, Aug. 8, 88 (actual)		05877
Last meter reading, July 8,88 (actual)	−	05524
Amount of electricity used	KWH	353

Current charges for 31 days - residential service (Rate 1)

Basic service charge (not including usage)	$	6.06
Charge for 353 KWH @ 6.9065 c each KWH	+	24.38
Fuel adjustment @ .1526 c each KWH	+	.54
Power purchase credit @ .0187 c each KWH	−	.07
Total cost for electric service	**$**	**30.91**

Gas Service

This meter reading, Aug. 8, 88 (actual)		3355
Last meter reading, July, 8, 88 (actual)	−	3334
Amount of gas used	CCF	21
Conversion to therms @ 1.02843 each CCF		22

Current charges for 31 days - residential service (Rate 1)

Basic service charge (first 3.10 therms)	$	5.80
Next 18.90 therms @ 66.8783 c each therm	+	12.64
Gas refund credit	−	.24
Gas adjustment @ 7.5492 c each therm	−	1.66
Total cost for gas service	**$**	**16.54**

Your energy use and cost

☒ = *Actual reading*

☑ = *Estimated reading*

▥ = *Customer reading*

☐ = *Average customer*

These charts show your energy use pattern over the last 13 months. They also show the current month's usage by our average residential customer.

KWH
A S O N D J F M A M J J A
8 7   8 8

Daily Averages:

	Last year	This period
Temp	74°	76°
KWH	10.3	11.4
Cost	$ .89	1.00
Therms	1.0	.7
Cost	$ .70	.53

Therms
A S O N D J F M A M J J A
8 7   8 8

(Reduced from original copy.)

41

Document Level 4 326-375
JTPA	ES/UI	Young Adults
12.2%	18.5%	24.0%

The tasks near the 350 level on the document scale (between 326 and 375 or Level 4) continue to demand more from the reader. Not only is proficiency needed in multiple-feature matching and integrating information from complex displays, as in Level 3, but the degree of inferencing required by the reader increases by Level 4 as well. For example, a task (RP80 of 327) that borders on the previous level directs the reader to use the pediatric medicine dosage chart shown earlier in this section. This particular task directs the reader to determine from the chart how much syrup is recommended for a child who is 10 years old and weighs 50 pounds. This task is difficult because one cannot simply match literal or synonymous information to perform successfully since the weight as given in the question is less than that of the typical 10-year-old in the table. Instead, one must rely on prior knowledge, or find the asterisked note relating to the column headed "Approximate Weight Range," that the correct dosage is to be based on weight (not age) to ensure that the child receives an effective dose. In any event, if the reader approaches this task as a single literal match, the age of the child is a highly plausible distractor and may lead to an incorrect response.

A more difficult task falling at the 364 level asks the reader to use charts and numerical entries that are part of a monthly bill from El Paso Gas and Electric. The reader is directed to write a brief statement describing how the customer's current month's use of kilowatt-hours compares with the average residential customer's use during the same month. Only the requisite portion of the bill is reproduced here on page 41. The reader's task was made substantially more difficult since the assessment instrument included two full pages of information constituting the actual monthly bill. The reader needs to identify the appropriate bar graph from among several presented and then integrate information to provide an appropriate response.

Individuals who perform in the Level 4 range on the document scale are estimated to demonstrate performance on more than 85 percent of the document tasks contained in this assessment with at least an 80 percent chance of success.

Document Level 5 ≥ 376
JTPA	ES/UI	Young Adults
1.1%	2.4%	4.1%

Tasks above 375 (or in Level 5) on this scale require readers to make broad text-based inferences or require specialized background knowledge that may involve using

Spotlight Economy

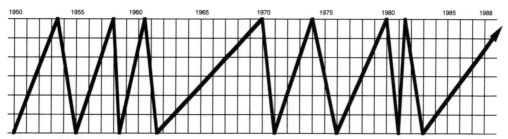

Business Cycles: From trough to peak, the current expansion is the second-longest economic recovery in post-war history.
Source: Data provided by Grace Messner, vice president and director of research, Wilmington Trust Co., and economist Richard Stuckey

The dollar vs. foreign currency

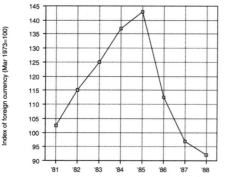

From 1981 to 1985, the dollar climbed sharply against the currencies of 10 industrialized countries before beginning its descent to 1988 levels.

U.S. imports, exports

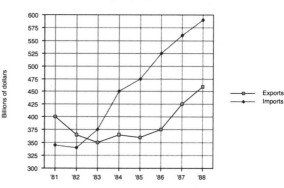

U.S. exports have trailed imports by a wide margin since 1982 when the strength of the dollar first began to boost the cost of American goods on world markets.

Interest rates

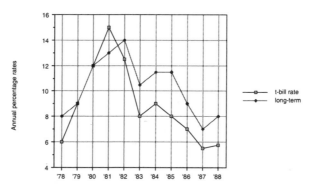

Short-term rates such as the three-month Treasury bill rate have not gone above the long-term rates on such instruments as 10-year bonds since the last recession.

(Reduced from original copy.)

multiple documents. For example, one task (RP80 of 386) directs the reader to locate the line graph depicting business cycles from among four graphs shown and to identify the periods that represent the longest and shortest economic recoveries. To respond correctly, readers need to process printed information under the graph in order to identify the appropriate graph and, in addition, to identify which lines represent economic recoveries. They must then compare this information with the lines provided in the graph to determine which periods represent economic recoveries. Then the reader must determine the longest and shortest and associate these with the specified time periods.

Individuals who are estimated to be performing at this highest level on the document scale demonstrate a broad range of skills at being able to process information with a high degree of consistency using a wide range of document materials that are drawn from various adult contexts. The tasks along the document scale range from those that require the reader to provide simple background information or to match on a single feature in simple well-labeled documents, to tasks that require the reader to use inferencing skills or background knowledge in connection with more complex displays in which information is embedded or not well identified.

Profiling Proficiencies on the Document Scale

Table 2.3 summarizes data about each of the five proficiency levels defined along the document scale. Starting at the left side of the table, the first column defines the range of each level on a 500-point scale, the second column provides a brief description of the processing demands associated with each level, and the third column contains the average RP80 value across the tasks located within a particular level, followed by columns displaying the average probability of getting these tasks correct at selected levels of proficiency. To understand how to interpret this information, it will be useful to look at an example that focuses on a particular proficiency level and the associated probabilities of responding correctly for individuals with different levels of proficiency. The third column shows that the average RP80 value of tasks falling within Level 3 (between 276 and 325 on the document scale) is 300. The figures to the right of this column show that someone with an estimated proficiency level of 200 is expected to answer the average Level 3 task correctly with a probability of 30 percent — that is, only about three out of 10 times. In contrast, someone estimated to have a proficiency of 250 would be expected to answer these types of tasks correctly 54 percent of the time while someone with a proficiency of 300 would be expected, on average, to have a 79 percent chance of responding correctly to Level 3 tasks. Now consider the probability of an individual with a proficiency level of 250 successfully performing tasks at each of the five levels. Figures in the column headed 250 indicate that such a person has a 94 percent chance of responding correctly to Level 1 tasks. This probability drops to only 81 percent for Level 2 tasks, 54 percent for Level 3 tasks, 26 percent for Level 4 tasks, and 23 percent for Level 5 tasks on the document scale.

The data displayed on the right side of Table 2.3 depict the percentages of JTPA and ES/UI populations estimated to be performing within each of the five levels on the document literacy scale. For comparison, similar information is also presented from the 1985 young adult literacy assessment. As with the prose scale, these percentages are presented for the total populations as well as for race/ethnicity and level of education.

Total Populations

As shown in Table 2.3, although there are some differences in the distributions between JTPA and ES/UI applicants, the two DOL populations differ significantly from the young adult population at each of the five levels. That is, the DOL populations have a significantly larger percentage of individuals at Levels 1 and 2 than do the young adults. For example, 14 percent of the JTPA and 13 percent of the ES/UI participants are at Level 1 as compared with 8 percent of young adults. Since these individuals demonstrate proficiency with document tasks requiring either entering personal background information or making a literal one-feature match, it would seem their literacy skills would place the most severe restrictions on their full participation in our increasingly complex society. They are estimated to be able to perform consistently about 25 percent of the tasks represented in this assessment on the document scale. It should be pointed out that a larger percentage of document tasks than prose tasks in this assessment are located within this first level. In addition, as noted in Section 3 of this report, persons at this level are performing at or below the level of those DOL respondents who report not attaining more than an eighth-grade education.

As with Level 1, when compared with the young adult population, a significantly larger percentage of each DOL population is performing at Level 2. There are 37 percent of the JTPA applicants and 30 percent of the ES/UI participants as compared with 24 percent of young adults. At this level, individuals can be expected to locate information based on more than one feature. Tasks at this level also begin to require the reader to compare and contrast information. Individuals scoring in Level 2 demonstrate a broader set of information-processing skills in that they can be expected to perform consistently about 60 percent of the document literacy tasks

Table 2.3	Document Literacy*									

Levels	Description of Document Tasks at Each of Five Levels	Average RP 80 at Each Level	Average Probability at Selected Proficiency Levels							TOTAL
			200	250	300	350	400			
Level 1 0-225	Tasks at this level are the least demanding. In general, they require the reader to either locate a piece of information based on a literal match or to enter information from personal knowledge.	194	80	94	98	100	100	JTPA ES/UI Young Adults		14.1 (2.0) 13.1 (1.6) 8.0 (0.6)
Level 2 226-275	Tasks at this level begin to become more varied. Some still require the reader to match a single piece of information; however, tasks occur where there are several distractors or where the match is based on low-level inferences. Tasks at this level also begin to require the reader to cycle through information or to integrate information	248	47	81	95	99	100	JTPA ES/UI Young Adults		37.3 (1.3) 30.1 (1.2) 24.2 (1.1)
Level 3 276-325	Tasks at this level tend to require the reader to either integrate three pieces of information or to cycle through materials in rather complex tables or graphs in which distractor information is present.	300	30	54	79	93	97	JTPA ES/UI Young Adults		35.4 (1.5) 35.9 (1.0) 39.7 (1.2)
Level 4 326-375	Tasks at this level continue to demand more from the reader. Not only are multiple-feature matching, cycling, and integration of information maintained, the degree of inferencing is increased. Cycling tasks often require the reader to make five or more responses with no designation of the correct number of responses. Condtitional information is also present and must be taken into account.	351	11	26	53	79	83	JTPA ES/UI Young Adults		12.2 (1.8) 18.5 (1.7) 24.0 (1.1)
Level 5 376-500	Tasks at this level require the most from the reader. The reader must search through complex displays contain multiple distractors, make high text-based inferences, or use specialized knowledge.	405	15	23	37	60	79	JTPA ES/UI Young Adults		1.1 (0.4) 2.4 (0.5) 4.1 (0.6)

*The numbers in parentheses are estimated standard errors.

	RACE/ETHNICITY			EDUCATION				
White	Black	Hispanic	0-8	9-12 No Dip.	H.S. Dip. or GED	Some Postsec.	College Degree
8.4 (1.2)	26.7 (4.0)	26.2 (5.2)	42.7 (4.0)	26.4 (3.8)	8.1 (1.3)	3.9 (0.9)	0.0 (0.0)
4.6 (0.7)	28.6 (4.4)	31.1 (3.2)	65.1(11.5)	32.9 (3.4)	11.2 (1.1)	5.6 (1.2)	3.6 (1.4)
4.3 (0.5)	25.6 (2.3)	15.0 (2.0)	60.8(12.7)	30.3 (2.6)	7.6 (0.8)	2.7 (0.6)	0.6 (0.3)
33.9 (1.8)	47.4 (2.4)	46.4 (5.3)	44.1 (4.8)	45.5 (2.2)	35.3 (1.8)	34.4 (3.1)	12.9 (5.0)
24.7 (1.5)	46.8 (5.2)	37.8 (1.1)	22.6 (5.8)	38.0 (2.0)	36.1 (2.0)	27.4 (1.2)	17.7 (2.2)
20.0 (1.1)	43.6 (2.0)	35.2 (3.3)	22.5 (5.0)	41.9 (2.8)	34.1 (1.7)	17.2 (2.0)	7.9 (1.3)
40.3 (1.7)	23.6 (2.6)	20.9 (5.3)	12.9 (4.2)	24.8 (4.3)	41.3 (1.7)	43.7 (2.8)	41.2 (5.7)
41.4 (1.1)	22.0 (3.1)	25.7 (3.9)	12.0 (9.6)	25.7 (3.0)	37.2 (2.1)	39.8 (3.1)	39.1 (5.8)
42.6 (1.5)	26.1 (1.8)	34.5 (3.2)	15.1(10.5)	23.6 (3.1)	45.9 (1.9)	41.5 (2.0)	36.6 (2.3)
15.8 (2.1)	2.3 (1.2)	6.4 (3.8)	0.3 (0.3)	3.4 (1.2)	14.0 (2.3)	16.8 (2.3)	39.7 (7.1)
25.7 (1.3)	2.6 (0.7)	4.7 (3.7)	0.4 (0.4)	3.3 (1.2)	14.1 (1.6)	25.2 (2.5)	32.5 (2.7)
28.0 (1.4)	4.7 (0.7)	14.2 (3.0)	1.6 (1.6)	4.0 (1.1)	11.4 (1.1)	33.5 (2.4)	44.1 (2.8)
1.6 (0.5)	0.0 (0.0)	0.1 (0.1)	0.0 (0.0)	0.0 (0.0)	1.2 (0.8)	1.1 (0.6)	6.1 (2.9)
3.6 (1.1)	0.0 (0.0)	0.7 (0.7)	0.0 (0.0)	0.1 (0.1)	1.4 (0.3)	2.0 (0.6)	7.1 (3.3)
5.1 (0.7)	0.1 (0.1)	1.1 (0.5)	0.0 (0.0)	0.1 (0.1)	1.0 (0.4)	5.1 (1.0)	10.8 (1.8)

contained in this assessment. However, those with demonstrated proficiency in the Level 2 range would still appear to be limited with respect to their ability to participate fully in our society. Moreover, as indicated in Section 3 of this report, these individuals are, on average, performing at about the level of individuals in the DOL populations who report dropping out of high school before earning a diploma.

Beginning at Level 3, the trend reverses and there is a larger proportion of young adults than either of the two DOL populations. Roughly 35 percent of each of the DOL populations demonstrate skills in this range (276 to 325) compared with 40 percent of the young adults. Such individuals demonstrate consistent success in dealing with three or more features of information from rather complex tables or graphs in which distracting information is present in the same row or column. These individuals can be expected to perform successfully on some 85 percent of the document tasks contained in this assessment. Although there is room for improvement, it is likely that these individuals are not experiencing major difficulty in using documents they encounter most frequently in their work and everyday lives. In fact, these individuals are performing at or above the level of JTPA and ES/UI program participants who report earning a high school diploma or GED.

As is the case with performance at Level 3 on the document scale, significantly larger percentages of young adults are at Levels 4 and 5 as compared with either the JTPA or ES/UI populations. Some 12 to 19 percent of the DOL populations are estimated to be performing at Level 4 compared with almost 25 percent of young adults. Similarly, only 1 to 2 percent of JTPA and ES/UI respondents are found at Level 5 compared with 4 percent of young adults. Individuals at this level are succeeding on 90 percent or more of the tasks contained on the document scale. These tasks require the reader to make high text-based inferences or to use specialized knowledge to contrast information. These tasks are above the average proficiency levels of DOL respondents who report a two-year college degree or higher.

Race/Ethnicity

The entries in Table 2.3 show an interesting pattern at Levels 1 and 2 for the different racial/ethnic subgroups. There are significantly higher percentages of White and Hispanic JTPA applicants scoring at Level 1 than White and Hispanic young adults. That is, almost twice the percentage of White and Hispanic JTPA eligible applicants as young adults demonstrate proficiency at Level 1. No significant differences appear between Black JTPA applicants and young adults at either Level 1 or 2.

In contrast, the most notable and highly significant difference for ES/UI populations is that at Level 1 the percentage of Hispanic ES/UI applicants is slightly more than twice that of Hispanic young adults. There are no differences for White and Black ES/UI participants at Level 1 in relation to young adults, while at Level 2 the only significant difference is that there is a higher percentage of White participants than young adults (25 compared with 20, respectively).

Although the patterns of statistical significance differ among the JTPA and ES/UI populations as compared with young adults, the general tendencies are the same. Higher percentages of JTPA and ES/UI program participants score in Levels 1 and 2, while a smaller percentage of each racial/ethnic group in the DOL populations demonstrates proficiencies at the three higher levels when compared with young adults.

Levels of Education

By and large, the JTPA distributions of document proficiency for each of the levels of education are notably similar to those for young adults. The exception is for those JTPA eligible applicants reporting some postsecondary experience, where smaller percentages of JTPA applicants than young adults attain Levels 4 and 5.

For ES/UI participants reporting less than a high school diploma or GED — within the ranges of zero to eight years and nine to 12 years of education — there are no significant differences as compared with similar distributions for young adults. The pattern of comparisons is different, however, for those reporting higher levels of educational attainment. Those ES/UI participants reporting higher levels of education — i.e., some postsecondary and college degree — have higher percentages of individuals at both Levels 1 and 2 than do young adults reporting similar levels of education. Moreover, of those ES/UI participants who report the two highest levels of education, lower percentages attain Levels 4 and 5 on the document scale than do comparable groups of young adults. Of the four possible comparisons, the only difference that does not reach at least the .05 level of significance is that for ES/UI participants who report a college degree or higher. It is not unreasonable to hypothesize that despite reported levels of education, low demonstrated literacy skills might be a contributing factor to the apparent difficulties ES/UI participants experience in the labor force.

Along this same line of reasoning, it is alarming to find that between 40 and 50 percent of each of the three populations who report earning a high school diploma or GED demonstrate skills limited to Levels 1 and 2. Conversely, only between 12 and 15 percent of each group of respondents demonstrate skills defined by Levels 4 and 5.

● Quantitative Literacy

The quantitative literacy scale used in this assessment contains 42 tasks that range from 226 to 422 on the scale. To complete these tasks successfully, a respondent must perform arithmetic operations such as addition, subtraction, multiplication, or division, either singly or in combination, using numbers or quantities that are embedded in printed information.

While at first glance the inclusion of quantitative tasks might appear to extend the concept of literacy beyond its traditional limits, an analysis of tasks along this scale shows that the processing of printed information plays a critical role in affecting the difficulty of these quantitative tasks. In general, it appears that many individuals can perform simple arithmetic operations when both the numbers and operations are made explicit. However, when these same operations are performed on numbers that must be located and extracted from different types of documents that contain similar but irrelevant information, or when these operations must be inferred from printed directions, the tasks become increasingly difficult.

As a result, the placement of tasks along this scale seems to be a function of:

● the particular arithmetic operation called for;

● the number of operations needed to perform the task;

● the extent to which the numbers are embedded in printed materials; and,

● the extent to which an inference must be made to identify the type of operation to perform.

Characterizing Levels of Proficiency on the Quantitative Scale

The following discussion highlights some of the tasks along the quantitative scale and describes how their placement along the scale seems to be affected by various combinations of the variables listed above. Throughout the discussion, the numbers associated with specific tasks refer to their location on the scale.

Quantitative Level **1** ≤ 225

JTPA	ES/UI	Young Adults
14.5%	11.7%	7.5%

Although no quantitative tasks used in this assessment fall below the score value of 225, experience suggests that such tasks would require the reader to perform a single, relatively simple arithmetic operation (e.g., addition or subtraction) for which either the numbers are already entered onto the given document and the operation is specified or the numbers are provided and the operation does not require the reader to borrow or carry.

Quantitative Level $\boxed{2}$ 226-275
JTPA   **ES/UI**   **Young Adults**
31.1%   25.3%   23.8%

The least demanding task on the quantitative scale requires the reader to enter and total two numbers on a bank deposit slip (RP80 of 226). In this instance, both the numbers and the operation are judged to be easily identified, and the operation involves the simple addition of two decimal numbers that are set up in column format and do not require carrying. Moreover, the numbers are stated in the question so the problem is, in some sense, defined for the reader.

In other tasks having similar characteristics that are somewhat higher on the scale, the quantities, while easy to identify, are not explicitly given in the question so the reader must search for and identify them in the document. One such task at the 265 level requires the reader to locate the appropriate shipping charges in a table before entering the correct amount on an order form and then to calculate the total price for ordering office supplies by adding a column of five dollar amounts.

■

NATIONAL BANK			Dollars	Cents
		CASH		
(Please Print)	Please use your personalized deposit tickets. If you need more, see your personal banker.	CHECKS List Singly		
Name _____		BE SURE EACH ITEM IS PROPERLY ENDORSED		
_____ 19 ____				
	Total Items	**TOTAL**		

CHECKS AND OTHER ITEMS ARE RECEIVED FOR DEPOSIT SUBJECT TO THE PROVISIONS OF THE UNIFORM COMMERCIAL CODE OR ANY APPLICABLE COLLECTION AGREEMENT.

(Reduced from original copy.)

■

Individuals who are estimated to be performing around 250 on the quantitative scale can be expected to perform tasks in the 226 to 275 range (Level 2) with about an 80 percent probability. The chance of performing tasks at the 276 to 325 level drops to just under 50 percent, while for the tasks above the 325 level the probabilities of success are 20 percent or less. That is, while they may be expected to respond correctly to tasks at these higher levels, they will most likely do so in an inconsistent manner. (See Table 2.4 for references to probabilities of success at various levels on the quantitative scale.)

Quantitative Level 3 276-325

JTPA	ES/UI	Young Adults
37.1%	37.4%	40.2%

Tasks around 300 (from 276 to 325, Level 3) on the quantitative scale still require a single operation of either addition, subtraction, multiplication, or division. What appears to distinguish these tasks, however, is the fact that the reader must identify two or more numbers from various places in the document needed to solve the problem. Also, the operation needed to complete the task is not explicitly stated in the directive or provided by the format of the document, as in the previous examples. Instead, the operation must be determined from arithmetic relation terms used in the question, such as "how many" or "what is the difference." For example, a task at the 283 level directs the reader to look at a table of money rates to determine, "How much higher was Thursday's prime lending rate as compared to the rate of one year ago?"

Another example of a task in this Level 3 range of complexity involves using an advertisement to determine the amount of savings over the retail price (RP80 of 302). To respond correctly to this task, the reader must identify the appropriate prices from a table by matching several pieces of information. The reader must then infer the appropriate operation from the phrase, "How much would you save," and perform the calculation correctly using the numbers identified.

Individuals who are estimated to be performing at about the 300 level successfully perform these types of quantitative tasks about 80 percent of the time. They have at least a 90 percent probability of correctly completing tasks below the 275 level. Their success on tasks between 326 and 375 drops to about 50 percent and to about 25 percent on tasks above the 375 level.

MONEY RATES

	Thurs.	6 mo. ago	Yr. ago
Prime lending	10.00%	8.50%	8.75%
Fed discount	6.50%	6.00%	6.00%
Broker call loan	9.13%	7.63%	8.13%
Mortgage rates			
30-yr. fixed-rate (FHLMC)	10.65%	9.85%	10.63%
30-yr. adjustable (FHLMC)	8.16%	7.53%	7.84%
15-yr. fixed rate[1]	10.39%	9.75%	10.28%
ARM index (1-year Treas.)	8.24%[2]	6.63%	7.41%
Money market accounts, latest 7-day average			
Money mutual funds[3]	7.37%	6.05%	6.03%
Banks and S&Ls[4]	5.81%	5.59%	5.47%
Treasury security rates			
3-month T-bill discount[4]	7.26%	5.74%	6.45%
6-month T-bill discount[4]	7.40%	5.93%	6.72%
7-year note	8.85%,-.01	8.12%	9.22%
30-year bond	9.03%, -.03	8.55%	9.57%

1—Bank Rate Monitor 2—week ending Sept. 2
3—Donoghue's Money Fund Report 4—Sept. 6 auction

THE DOLLAR

(Reduced from original copy.)

BusinessLand says they offer discount prices. If you purchased 1 narrow-with-slot printer stand, how much would you save by paying BusinessLand's price rather than the retail price?

BUSINESSLAND PRINTER STAND

Save space with our economical printer stand.
We wanted to prove a printer stand could perform perfectly, look good and still not cost much. So we commissioned this handsome, smoky grey acrylic stand. It's a convenient, inexpensive desktop solution. It keeps your printer paper stacked and ready without taking up extra desk space. Your paper feeds smoothly into your printer because it's tucked conveniently underneath. Also available with center slot for bottom feed printers. Comes in two sizes to fit either 80 or 132 column paper. Order this inexpensive space saver today.

BUSINESSLAND PRINTER STAND

DESCRIPTION		ORDER NO.	RETAIL	QTY. 1	QTY. 2-4
Narrow	15"W x 12"D x 4-1/2"H - 80 column	475-5231	$24.95	$22.95	$18.95
Narrow w/slot	15"W x 12"D x 4-1/2"H - 80 column	475-5447	$25.95	$23.95	$19.95
Wide	20"W x 12"D x 4-1/2"H - 132 column	475-5249	$34.95	$22.70	$22.70
Wide w/slot	20"W x 12"D x 4-1/2"H - 132 column	475-5462	$35.95	$22.95	$22.95
Printer Stand for HP ThinkJet		462-41152	$49.95	$48.95	$38.95

(Reduced from original copy.)

Quantitative Level ▮4▮ 326-375

JTPA	ES/UI	Young Adults
15.1%	21.4%	24.0%

Tasks around 350 (between 326 and 375, Level 4) tend to require two or more sequential operations or the application of a single operation where either the quantities or the operation is not easily determined. For example, one task at the 331 level directs the reader to use a flight information table to determine the latest plane that a visitor could take from a particular city to arrive in time for a meeting, given a set of conditions spelled out in the directive.

■

FROM DENVER				FROM MINNEAPOLIS			
Flight #	Departure	Arrival	Meal	Flight #	Departure	Arrival	Meal
605	6:05	7:10	B	352	6:15	8:35	S
397	7:45	8:50	B	498	7:10	9:40	B
552	8:00	9:05	S	176	7:30	10:15	B
782	8:30	9:45	S	544	8:05	10:45	S
310	9:00	10:10	S	386	9:10	11:30	S
170	10:05	11:15	S	904	9:45	12:15 p.m.	S
451	10:30	11:40	S	881	10:00	12:10	S
893	11:45	12:50 p.m.	S	455	10:30	12:45	S
116	12:15 p.m.	1:20	L	254	11:45	2:15	L
789	2:30	3:45	S	562	12:30 p.m.	3:40	S
245	3:50	5:10	S	784	2:50	5:50	S
436	5:30	6:45	D	895	4:15	6:55	D
576	6:05	7:15	S	902	5:45	8:20	D
776	8:45	9:55	S	114	6:00	8:40	D
002	10:15	11:20	S	008	7:20	10:00	S

(Reduced from original copy.)

■

In this instance, the quantities to be used are easily identified from the directive; however, the respondent must infer the appropriate operations from the semantic information given or from prior knowledge. No arithmetic relation terms are provided, such as "how much" or "what is the difference."

A slightly more difficult task on this scale (RP80 of 354) directs the reader to use a graph to "estimate the difference between short-term and long-term interest rates at the beginning of 1985." In this example, only one operation is required, and it is easily inferred from the terms used in the directive. What appears to contribute to the task's difficulty is that the appropriate graph must be identified from among four presented and then the two quantities identified. While one of the points to be compared falls on a numbered line in the graph, the other must be interpolated from the information provided.

Individuals who perform at Level 4 on this scale have roughly an 80 percent probability of responding correctly to the types of tasks described in this 326 to 375 range. They can be expected, on average, to complete successfully quantitative tasks falling below the 326 level with a better than 95 percent probability.

Quantitative Level **5** ≥ 376

JTPA	ES/UI	Young Adults
2.2%	4.2%	4.6%

Tasks surpassing 375, Level 5, tend either to have conditional information that requires the reader to disembed appropriate features of a problem from various parts of the document or to require the reader to draw heavily on background information in order to identify both the quantities and the operations needed to complete the task successfully. For example, a task at the 406 level on the quantitative scale asks the reader, "How much will it cost to enroll in a 4-credit biology class with a lab if you register on time and are NOT a senior citizen?" The most difficult task on this scale (RP80 of 422) requires readers to look at an advertisement for a home equity loan and then, using the information provided, explain how they would calculate the total amount of interest charges associated with the loan.

■

FIXED RATE • FIXED TERM

HOME EQUITY LOANS **14.25%**
Annual Percentage Rate
Ten Year Term

SAMPLE MONTHLY REPAYMENT SCHEDULE

Amount Financed	Monthly Payment
$10,000	$156.77
$25,000	$391.93
$40,000	$627.09

120 Months 14.25% APR

■

Individuals who are estimated to be performing above the 375 level demonstrate the highest level of proficiency on the quantitative scale. As such, they exhibit skill in using the basic arithmetic operations in conjunction with a broad variety of printed materials.

Profiling Proficiencies on the Quantitative Scale

Table 2.4 summarizes data about each of the five proficiency levels defined along the quantitative scale. Starting at the left side of the table, the first column defines the range of each level on a 500-point scale, the second column provides a brief description of the processing demands associated with each level, and the third column contains the average RP80 value across the tasks located within a particular level, followed by columns displaying the average probability of getting these tasks correct at selected levels of proficiency. To understand how to interpret this information, it will be useful to look at an example that focuses on a particular proficiency level and the associated probabilities of responding correctly for individuals with different levels of proficiency. The third column shows that the average RP80 value of tasks falling within Level 3 (between 276 and 325 on the quantitative scale) is 299. The figures to the right of this column show that someone with an estimated proficiency level of 200 is expected to answer the average Level 3 task correctly with a probability of 17 percent — that is, less than two out of 10 times. In contrast, someone estimated to have a proficiency of 250 would be expected to answer these types of tasks correctly 45 percent of the time, while someone with a proficiency of 300 would be expected, on average, to have an 81 percent chance of responding correctly to Level 3 tasks. Now consider the probability of an individual with a proficiency level of 250 successfully performing tasks at each of the five levels. Figures in the column headed 250 indicate that such a person has a 76 percent chance of responding correctly to Level 2 tasks. This probability drops to only 45 percent for Level 3 tasks, 20 percent for Level 4 tasks, and 11 percent for Level 5 tasks.

The data displayed on the right side of Table 2.4 depict the percentages of JTPA and ES/UI populations estimated to be performing within each of the five levels on the quantitative literacy scale. For comparison, similar information is also presented from the 1986 young adult literacy assessment. As with the prose and document scales, these percentages are presented for the total populations as well as for race/ethnicity and level of education.

Total Populations

Although the two DOL populations differ somewhat from each other along the five levels of proficiency, it is primarily the JTPA population that differs from the distributions of young adults shown in Table 2.4 for the quantitative scale. Significantly larger percentages of JTPA eligible applicants perform at Levels 1 and 2 than do young adults, while significantly smaller percentages attain Levels 4 and 5. No difference appears at Level 3 between JTPA applicants and young adults. Only the difference at Level 1 between ES/UI participants and young adults reaches statistical significance: some 12 to 15 percent of JTPA and ES/UI respondents are estimated to be performing in the range of Level 1 tasks compared with 8 percent of young adults.

Although no quantitative tasks used in this assessment fell within this range, experience suggests that tasks at Level 1 would require addition or subtraction in which either the numbers are already entered on a form in column format or the operation does not require the reader to borrow or carry. It would seem, therefore, that literacy skills of those respondents estimated to be performing at Level 1 would place the most severe restrictions on their full participation in society. As noted in Section 3 of this report, they are performing at or below the level of those individuals who report zero to eight years of education.

Roughly 25 to 30 percent of the applicants in each of these populations are estimated to score in the Level 2 range on the quantitative scale. At this level, individuals can be expected to perform a single arithmetic operation involving numbers that are either stated in the question or easily identified in the document. Demonstrated proficiency in this range appears to be a limiting factor since individuals scoring in Level 2 demonstrate consistent performance on only three tasks representing fewer than 10 percent of the quantitative tasks used in this assessment. Moreover, as indicated in to Section 3 in this report, these individuals are, on average, performing at about the level of those who report dropping out of school before earning a high school diploma or GED.

As shown in Table 2.4, nearly 40 percent of each population demonstrate performance in the Level 3 range. Such individuals demonstrate consistent success in dealing with tasks in which two or more numbers needed to solve the problem must be identified in different places in the document or text. In addition, the operation(s) needed to complete the task are determined from arithmetic relation terms such as "how many" or "what is the difference" given in the question or directive. These individuals can be expected to perform successfully (with some 80 percent probability or higher) 55 percent of the quantitative tasks contained in this assessment. Although there is room for improvement, it is likely that these individuals are not encountering

Table 2.4 Quantitative Literacy*

Levels	Description of Quantitative Tasks at Each of Five Levels	Average RP 80 at Each Level	Average Probability at Selected Proficiency Levels					TOTAL	
			200	250	300	350	400		
Level 1 0-225	Although no quantitative tasks used in this assessment fall within this level, experience suggests such tasks would require a single, relatively simple operation for which the numbers are given and the arithmetic operation specified.	**			**			JTPA ES/UI Young Adults	14.5 (1.4) 11.7 (1.9) 7.5 (0.7)
Level 2 226-275	Tasks at this level typically require the use of a single operation based on numbers that are either stated in the question or easily located in the material. In addition, the operation needed is either stated in the question or easily determined based on the format of the problem — for example, entries on a bank deposit slip or order form.	256	45	76	93	98	100	JTPA ES/UI Young Adults	31.1 (2.4) 25.3 (1.1) 23.8 (1.2)
Level 3 276-325	What appears to distinguish tasks at this level is that two or more numbers needed to solve the problem must be found in the stimulus material. Also the operation(s) needed can be determined from arithmetic relation terms.	299	17	45	81	95	99	JTPA ES/UI Young Adults	37.1 (1.7) 37.4 (1.3) 40.2 (1.1)
Level 4 326-375	Quantitative tasks at level 4 tend to require two or more sequential operations or the application of a single operation where either the quantities must be located in complex displays and/or the operations must be inferred from semantic information given or prior knowledge.	350	70	20	49	79	94	JTPA ES/UI Young Adults	15.1 (1.8) 21.4 (1.5) 24.0 (1.2)
Level 5 376-500	Quantitative tasks at this level are the most demanding. They tend to require the reader to perform multiple operations and to disembed features of a problem from stimulus material or to rely on background knolwedge to determine the quantities or operations needed.	408	5	11	28	54	77	JTPA ES/UI Young/Adults	2.2 (0.6) 4.2 (0.5) 4.6 (0.5)

* The numbers in parentheses are estimated standard errors.
** No tasks at this level

	RACE/ETHNICITY			EDUCATION				
White	Black	Hispanic	0-8	9-12 No Dip.	H.S. Dip. or GED	Some Postsec.	College Degree	
9.2 (1.0)	25.9 (3.2)	29.9 (4.8)	43.8 (5.4)	27.4 (1.8)	7.3 (1.1)	5.5 (2.0)	2.3 (2.2)
4.3 (0.9)	26.9 (5.6)	25.7 (3.7)	61.3(11.1)	30.1 (4.7)	9.1 (1.4)	4.9 (1.0)	4.0 (1.4)
4.2 (0.6)	24.9 (2.4)	15.9 (1.9)	31.6 (7.8)	30.5 (3.6)	8.4 (1.0)	1.9 (0.3)	0.4 (0.2)
27.0 (2.2)	42.1 (3.6)	30.6 (5.3)	35.3 (6.2)	41.6 (2.9)	30.2 (3.2)	22.7 (2.6)	6.3 (2.4)
18.4 (0.8)	36.5 (3.9)	40.6 (2.8)	33.5(10.0)	39.5 (4.2)	26.8 (1.6)	24.0 (1.4)	11.8 (1.5)
20.2 (1.2)	39.6 (1.7)	33.7 (3.7)	33.8 (7.3)	37.2 (2.9)	29.7 (1.9)	19.3 (1.8)	12.4 (2.1)
41.3 (1.8)	26.5 (2.6)	30.2 (5.3)	20.5 (4.1)	25.0 (2.8)	43.3 (2.6)	51.2 (3.4)	24.8 (8.4)
42.1 (0.8)	31.7 (6.5)	26.6 (3.6)	5.3 (1.9)	25.7 (3.3)	44.3 (2.1)	42.6 (1.3)	31.2 (3.6)
42.6 (1.2)	26.8 (2.3)	35.3 (3.4)	34.6 (9.3)	27.5 (3.2)	42.9 (1.9)	43.1 (1.8)	37.9 (2.1)
19.3 (1.8)	5.2 (1.8)	9.3 (3.0)	0.4 (0.3)	6.0 (2.0)	17.4 (2.3)	18.7 (2.8)	46.1 (5.9)
29.0 (0.9)	4.8 (1.4)	7.0 (0.8)	0.0 (0.0)	4.1 (1.4)	17.1 (1.5)	25.2 (1.9)	41.3 (3.6)
27.5 (1.3)	8.4 (1.7)	13.7 (3.1)	0.0 (0.0)	3.7 (0.9)	17.9 (1.7)	29.6 (1.8)	38.6 (2.9)
3.2 (0.8)	0.3 (0.2)	0.0 (0.0)	0.0 (0.0)	0.0 (0.0)	1.8 (0.6)	1.8 (0.9)	20.5 (7.0)
6.2 (0.8)	0.0 (0.0)	0.0 (0.0)	0.0 (0.0)	0.6 (0.5)	2.7 (0.8)	3.4 (0.5)	11.7 (2.5)
5.6 (0.6)	0.4 (0.2)	1.3 (0.6)	0.0 (0.0)	1.0 (1.0)	1.0 (0.3)	6.1 (1.0)	10.8 (1.6)

major difficulty in performing well-structured arithmetic problems that may be frequently associated with work and home. These individuals are performing at about the level of JTPA and ES/UI populations who report earning a high school diploma or GED.

About 20 to 30 percent of these three populations demonstrate skills at or above the Level 4 range. While 5 percent or less attain Level 5, as a group these individuals are succeeding on nearly 90 percent of the tasks contained on the quantitative scale. These tasks require the application of two or more sequential operations or the application of a single operation where either the numbers or the operation cannot easily be determined. The most challenging tasks require the reader to disembed appropriate features of a problem from various parts of the document or to rely heavily on background knowledge. These skills are commensurate with the skills of individuals who report a two-year college degree or higher.

Race/Ethnicity

When compared with the performance of Black young adults, there are no significant differences in the distributions for Black participants in each of the DOL programs. Except at Levels 1 and 5, there also are no differences between Hispanic JTPA applicants and Hispanic young adults. In contrast, significant differences are seen in the distributions of White JTPA applicants and White young adults except at Level 3. Larger percentages of White applicants are at Levels 1 and 2 — 9.2 and 27.0, respectively — compared with 4.2 and 20.2 for young adults. At Levels 4 and 5, 19 and 3 percent of White JTPA applicants are found compared with 28 and 6 percent of White young adults.

As with Black applicants within the two DOL programs, no differences emerge between the distributions of performance for White ES/UI participants and young adults. However, significantly larger percentages of Hispanic ES/UI participants are shown at Level 1, while smaller percentages of Hispanic participants are at Levels 4 and 5 when compared with similar subgroups of young adults. The corresponding percentages are 26 for ES/UI Hispanic participants at Level 1 as compared with 16 for Hispanic young adults. At Levels 4 and 5, the comparable percentages are 7 and 0 versus 14 and 1.

As with the prose and document scales, Black and Hispanic respondents in all three populations are disproportionately represented along the quantitative literacy scale when compared with White respondents. As displayed in Table 2.4, some 16 to 30 percent are estimated to be performing within Level 1 compared with only 4 to 9 percent of White adults. Conversely, while only some 5 to 10 percent of Black and

Hispanic adults demonstrate proficiency at Levels 4 and 5 on the quantitative scale, between 20 and 35 percent of White respondents attain these levels.

Levels of Education

The entries in Table 2.4 for the quantitative scale indicate considerably more similarities than differences among the three populations. The relatively few differences that do emerge are scattered across the various distributions for JTPA and ES/UI participants. The one notable exception is among ES/UI participants reporting some postsecondary education and a college degree. Generally, these groups are overrepresented at Levels 1 and 2 compared with young adults. This picture is very similar to that shown for the document scale.

Summary and Conclusions

The definition of literacy adopted for this study assumes that literacy involves the skills needed to do something rather than simply the knowledge of something. While knowledge is important, the emphasis here is on literacy as a tool which enables people to participate more fully at work, at home, and in their communities. Literacy skills allow individuals to use printed and written information so they are able, among other things, to participate in local and national government, to hold and advance in a job, to understand and obtain legal and community services, to manage a household, as well as to improve themselves.

In pursuing these activities, people interact with many different types of printed materials for different purposes. The resulting wide array of literacy behaviors is likely to require different types of skills and knowledge that are better represented as continua rather than as an all-or-nothing condition. While some studies have arbitrarily designated individuals into one of two categories — literate or illiterate — these terms are misleading in that, by themselves, they provide little guidance or understanding of the nature of the problem or the types of behaviors that could be helpful in addressing it.

Through the anchoring process described in this section of the report, specific prose, document, and quantitative tasks have been identified along each of the literacy scales. These tasks characterize the interactions between materials and questions or directives that appear to affect both the type and level of processing needed to respond correctly. These analyses suggest that there appears to be an ordered set of information-processing skills and strategies that may be called into play to accomplish the range of tasks represented in the various aspects of literacy defined here.

At the risk of oversimplification, we have attempted in Figure 2.1 to characterize these proficiencies in terms of five discrete levels described in this section, integrating across the three literacy scales.

Figure 2.1　Levels of Proficiency

LEVEL 1: Less Than or Equal to 225 on the Literacy Scales

Tasks falling within this range on the three literacy scales are the least demanding in terms of what a reader must do in order to produce a correct response. In general, prose and document tasks at this level require a reader to identify and enter information from personal knowledge or to locate a piece of information in which there is a literal match between the question and the stimulus material. If a distractor or plausible answer appears in the stimulus material, it tends to be located away from where the correct information is found. Although no quantitative tasks used in this assessment fell within this level, experience suggests that such tasks would require the reader to perform a single, relatively simple arithmetic operation (such as addition or subtraction) for which either the numbers are already entered onto the document and the operation is given or the numbers are provided and the operation does not require the reader to borrow or carry.

LEVEL 2: 226-275 on the Literacy Scales

Prose and document literacy tasks falling within this range are more varied in terms of the demands placed on readers. Some of these tasks still require the reader to locate and match on a single literal feature of information; however, these tasks tend to occur in materials in which there are several distractors or where the match is based on synonymous or text-based inferences. Prose and document tasks at Level 2 also begin to require readers to integrate information by either pulling together two pieces of information or by comparing and contrasting information. Quantitative tasks at this level typically require the use of one arithmetic operation based on numbers that are either stated in the question or easily located in the document through a literal one-feature match. Moreover, the operation needed to complete the task is either stated in the question or easily determined based on the format of the problem — for example, entries on a bank deposit slip or on an order form.

LEVEL 3: 276-325 on the Literacy Scales

Prose tasks at this level tend to require the reader to search fairly dense text for literal or synonymous matches on the basis of more than one feature of information or to integrate information from relatively long text that does not contain organizational aids such as headings. Document tasks at this level tend to require the reader to integrate three or more features of information from rather complex tables or graphs in which distractors are present in the same row or column. What appears to distinguish quantitative tasks at this level is the fact that two or more numbers or quantities needed to solve the problem must be identified from various places in the material. Also, the operation(s) needed to complete the task is typically determined from arithmetic relation terms in the question, such as "How many" or "What is the difference."

LEVEL 4: 326-375 on the Literacy Scales

Tasks in this range continue to demand more from the reader. Not only are multiple-feature matching and integration of information from complex materials maintained, the degree of inferencing required by the reader is also increased. Tasks at this level include conditional information that must be taken into account by the reader in order to integrate or match information appropriately. Quantitative tasks at Level 4 tend to require two or more sequential operations or the application of a single operation where either the quantities or the operation must be determined from the semantic information given or from prior knowledge.

LEVEL 5: 376 and Higher on the Literacy Scales

Tasks falling within this range tend to place the greatest demands on the reader. Typically, they require the reader to search for information in dense text or complex documents containing multiple plausible distractors, to make high text-based inferences or use specialized background knowledge, as well as to compare and contrast sometimes complex information to determine differences. Similarly, the quantitative tasks at this level require the reader to disembed features of a problem from various parts of a stimulus or to rely heavily on background knowledge to identify both the quantities and the operations needed to complete a task successfully.

SECTION 3

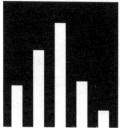

*T*his section explores differences in mean performance scores across the three literacy scales on the basis of several demographic, education, and labor-market variables. These include demographic variables of gender, age, and race/ethnicity, the variable of educational attainment, alternative high school certification, and two variables relating to labor market status — weeks of employment and whether or not participants were employed, unemployed and looking for work, or out of the labor force during the week prior to the assessment. Such data are important for understanding the extent and nature of any existing literacy problems and in determining how serious they are. Moreover, these data serve to establish baseline information against which changes can be measured over time.

● TOTAL *JTPA* AND *ES/UI* POPULATIONS

Table 3.1 indicates that the Employment Service and Unemployment Insurance (ES/UI) program participants score, on average, about 291 on the prose scale, 284 on the document scale, and 291 on the quantitative scale. These average proficiency scores are somewhat higher than those demonstrated by eligible applicants for the Job Training Partnership Act (JTPA) programs where the mean scores are 284, 274, and 281, respectively. These differences among group means are statistically significant (at the .05 level) for the document and quantitative scales but not for the prose scale.

	n	Weighted N	Prose	Document	Quantitative
Total JTPA	2,501	1,100,000	284.2 (2.9)	274.3 (3.1)	280.6 (3.1)
Males	1,008	451,859	274.3 (3.6)	270.7 (4.1)	278.4 (3.7)
Females	1,484	637,956	291.3 (2.9)	277.3 (2.8)	282.6 (3.1)
Total ES/UI	3,277	18,937,087	290.6 (4.0)	283.6 (3.1)	290.6 (3.1)
Males	1,756	10,631,408	287.0 (4.7)	282.5 (4.1)	291.5 (3.9)
Females	1,515	8,255,060	295.6 (3.6)	285.4 (3.1)	289.4 (2.9)

Table 3.1 — Weighted Average Proficiency Scores on the Three Literacy Scales by Population and Gender*

*The numbers in parentheses are estimated standard errors.

● MEN AND WOMEN

As can be seen from Table 3.1, the majority of the eligible JTPA applicants are female (58 percent) while the majority of ES/UI program participants are male (56 percent[1]). There is a tendency for women to perform somewhat higher than men, but in most instances, the differences are only a few points and are not statistically significant. For the JTPA population, however, women do score significantly higher than men on the prose scale, with the mean scores being 291 and 274, respectively.

These results are somewhat different from the findings given in the 1986 young adult literacy report. Although there was also a tendency for women to score somewhat higher than men on the prose scale (298 as compared with 295), this difference was not statistically significant. However, the National Assessment of Educational Progress has reported that elementary and secondary school girls have performed significantly better than boys on the NAEP reading scale across several assessments. It may be that the prose scale measures aspects of literacy that are the most sensitive to the reading curriculum taught in schools.

● AGE

Table 3.2 provides a summary of the relationship between demonstrated literacy proficiencies and age for the total JTPA and ES/UI populations. The modal (or most frequent) age group for the populations being served by each program is 32 to 45 years. Roughly one-third of the applicants in each program are in

---

[1] For some variables, there are missing data because not all respondents answered all the questions they should have in the background questionnaire. As a result, the numbers for a particular subgroup may not add up to the number for the total sample. Percents reported are for responding groups and are interpreted against appropriate total groups.

this age range. Nevertheless, the age distributions reveal that JTPA is serving a higher proportion of individuals in the combined 16-to-25 age ranges than is ES/UI (36 percent compared to 28 percent), while ES/UI is serving a higher proportion of adults 46 years and older than is JTPA (17 percent compared with 10 percent).

In the ES/UI population, individuals in the combined age ranges of 16 to 25 perform significantly below the levels of literacy demonstrated by other age groups, while it appears that literacy proficiencies are at similar levels across the three upper age groups. The picture is somewhat different for JTPA eligible applicants. Within this population, it is only individuals in the youngest age group (16 to 20) who demonstrate significantly lower levels of proficiency, although demonstrated proficiencies seem to drop off somewhat for those aged 46 and older.

Table 3.2	Weighted Average Proficiency Scores on the Three Literacy Scales by Population and Age*				
	n	Weighted N	Prose	Document	Quantitative
JTPA					
16-20	489	185,317	265.4 (3.1)	260.3 (4.5)	262.6 (3.0)
21-25	485	213,863	286.7 (3.5)	279.9 (3.4)	283.0 (3.7)
26-31	505	233,885	287.6 (5.4)	278.2 (3.8)	282.6 (4.1)
32-45	733	340,218	292.8 (3.3)	280.2 (5.1)	289.6 (5.0)
46+	259	115,018	280.8 (7.1)	263.8 (3.4)	277.4 (4.8)
ES/UI					
16-20	314	1,845,836	276.5 (7.6)	274.7 (4.3)	272.3 (4.1)
21-25	616	3,418,336	278.7 (4.7)	274.8 (6.0)	281.9 (5.8)
26-31	727	4,146,004	291.8 (4.1)	284.9 (3.3)	293.2 (3.3)
32-45	1,059	6,109,941	297.9 (5.1)	290.1 (3.2)	297.4 (3.2)
46+	546	3,308,221	297.0 (4.4)	284.4 (4.5)	294.2 (4.7)

*The numbers in parentheses are estimated standard errors.

● RACE/ETHNICITY

As shown in Table 3.3, race/ethnicity has a notable relationship with mean performance for both the JTPA and the ES/UI populations. The data in this table show Black and Hispanic program participants scoring significantly below White participants. Among ES/UI participants, the difference between minority and White participants is, on average, a full standard deviation (50 points on the 0 to 500 score scale). For JTPA eligible applicants, the difference is somewhat smaller (about 30 points or only 60 percent of a standard deviation) but, nevertheless, highly statistically significant.

According to these data, the Hispanic survey participants applying for JTPA and ES/UI benefits perform, on average, at about the same level as Black participants. This finding is in contrast to those from other national databases in which Hispanic populations typically have been reported to obtain mean scores about midway between White and Black groups, or roughly one-half standard deviation from each.[2] Since the Hispanic participants in ES/UI programs obtain mean scores that are at least a full standard deviation below that for White participants, it appears that ES/UI programs are serving a less proficient population of Hispanic participants than would be expected of a nationally representative sample of the total population. The same argument holds for Hispanic applicants for JTPA programs, but to a lesser degree. On the other hand, since the means for eligible Black applicants for JTPA are only some 60 percent of a standard deviation below that for White applicants, it appears that the self-selection bias operating here is for more proficient Black individuals to apply for JTPA services.

Table 3.3	Weighted Average Proficiency Scores on the Three Literacy Scales by Race/Ethnicity*

	n	Weighted N	Prose	Document	Quantitative
JTPA					
White	1,556	760,740	292.8 (2.8)	284.3 (2.9)	291.5 (2.5)
Black	663	230,405	264.1 (4.8)	250.5 (4.5)	255.6 (4.8)
Hispanic	159	64,912	263.0 (6.1)	251.7 (5.0)	258.0 (5.2)
ES/UI					
White	2,394	11,894,800	311.1 (1.8)	301.8 (2.0)	308.5 (1.5)
Black	375	2,189,197	261.7 (5.2)	250.7 (3.5)	257.9 (5.8)
Hispanic	384	3,824,079	249.6 (5.0)	246.1 (5.6)	254.0 (4.5)

*The numbers in parentheses are estimated standard errors.

It is particularly important to emphasize that these data do not imply that all minority group members score at the lower levels on the three literacy scales or that the cause for lower performance is to be explained by the race/ethnicity variable. For example, data from the High School and Beyond study indicate that Black and Hispanic students are overrepresented in the low socioeconomic status group, which includes about 54 percent of Black and 57 percent of Hispanic high school seniors.

---

[2] D. Rock, R. Ekstrom, M. Goertz, and J. Pollack. (1985). *Study of excellence in high school education: Longitudinal study, 1980-82*, (Princeton, NJ: Educational Testing Service.)
I. S. Kirsch and A. Jungeblut. (1986). *Literacy: Profiles of America's young adults*, (NAEP Report No. 16-PL-01), (Princeton, NJ: Educational Testing Service.)

The scores of high school seniors from disadvantaged backgrounds are consistently one standard deviation below the average scores of those students from advantaged backgrounds.[3] Moreover, recent data indicate that while as many as 20 percent of all children in this country may be growing up in homes that are at or near poverty levels, the percentage for minority populations could be as high as 50 percent.

● LEVELS OF EDUCATION

Each person participating in this study was asked to state how many years of formal education he or she had completed. For reporting purposes, responses to this question were categorized into zero to eight years; nine to 12 years but no diploma; a high school diploma or GED equivalency; some postsecondary; and, a two- or four-year college degree or higher. As the data in Table 3.4 show, there is a very strong, positive relationship between reported level of education and demonstrated proficiency on each of the three literacy scales for both the JTPA and ES/UI populations. The difference in proficiency scores is significant at each successive level of education with the magnitude of the difference between the highest and lowest levels of education being about 100 points or two standard deviations.

Table 3.4	Weighted Average Proficiency Scores on the Three Literacy Scales by Population and Level of Education*				
	n	Weighted N	Prose	Document	Quantitative
JTPA					
0-8 Years	176	64,975	232.3 (4.6)	231.5 (5.5)	233.9 (5.1)
9-12 Years	705	302,247	255.3 (2.7)	249.5 (4.4)	254.4 (3.1)
H.S. Dip. or GED	1,045	484,742	294.1 (3.3)	283.0 (3.0)	289.6 (2.1)
Some Postsec.	442	184,509	306.3 (3.1)	291.6 (3.2)	298.4 (4.1)
College Degree	130	61,480	339.3 (11.1)	321.1 (8.9)	336.9 (9.8)
ES/UI					
0-8 Years	120	511,432	196.4 (14.1)	199.8 (17.1)	211.0 (12.5)
9-12 Years	500	2,941,253	249.1 (7.0)	247.1 (5.1)	251.7 (4.5)
H.S. Dip. or GED	1,279	6,681,481	286.1 (2.1)	279.4 (1.8)	288.4 (2.7)
Some Postsec.	861	5,154,636	303.4 (3.9)	296.5 (2.5)	299.9 (2.5)
College Degree	513	3,601,479	328.8 (4.2)	315.1 (4.7)	324.6 (3.8)

*The numbers in parentheses are estimated standard errors.

---

[3] A. Sum, P. Harrington, and W. Goedicke. (1986). *Basic skills of America's teens and young adults: Findings of the 1980 national ASVAB testing and their implications for education, employment and training policies and programs*, (Boston, MA: Center for Labor Market Studies, Northeastern University.)

Given the billions of dollars spent on education in this country, it would be gratifying to interpret these differences in proficiencies as a sole result of the decision by some to continue their education, independent of other factors. Unfortunately, the relationship between educational attainment and literacy proficiency is not so simple. On the one hand, those who report staying in school longer do demonstrate higher levels of proficiency. On the other hand, it may be that those with higher levels of proficiency choose to stay in school longer. In addition, other demographic and background variables are likely to play an important role in helping to explain the variation noted here.

For example, data from the young adult literacy assessment indicate that intergenerational aspects of poor academic performance — parental education, economic situation, and early home experiences — are all likely to affect an individual's system of values and knowledge. These value and knowledge systems can be expected to have cumulative and lasting effects on interests, motivations, aspirations, and ultimately on literacy practices and proficiencies.

Table 3.4 reveals that ES/UI participants attain, on average, higher levels of education than those eligible for JTPA programs. For example, a larger percentage of ES/UI participants report having some type of college degree than do eligible JTPA applicants. In addition, among the total DOL populations, almost 20 percent of the ES/UI participants report not obtaining a high school diploma as compared with about 33 percent of JTPA eligible applicants. Except among applicants who report zero to eight years of education, the mean literacy proficiencies for the two DOL populations do not differ significantly on the basis of educational attainment. However, as would be expected, the mean proficiencies increase with higher reported educational attainment across scales within each population.

The strong relationship between level of education and literacy proficiency holds for each racial/ethnic subgroup within the JTPA and ES/UI populations. As shown in Table 3.5, regardless of racial/ethnic background, level of education is significantly related to level of performance on the three literacy scales. In addition, there are few mean performance differences between JTPA and ES/UI populations within a particular level of educational attainment. While a number of the differences in mean scores appear large, the only differences between JTPA and ES/UI means that are statistically significant at the .05 level or above for White respondents are found on the document scale for individuals reporting nine to 12 years of education (high school dropouts) and for those reporting some postsecondary experience. The only significant difference for Black program participants is on the document scale for individuals reporting zero to eight years of education.

Table 3.5	Weighted Average Proficiency Scores on the Three Literacy Scales by Race/Ethnicity and Level of Education*

JTPA Level of Education

Race/Ethnicity	0-8 Yrs.	9-12 Yrs.	H.S. Diploma or GED	Some Post-secondary	College Degree
White					
Prose	242.9 (6.9)	261.6 (3.7)	300.9 (3.6)	318.2 (3.8)	346.4 (13.2)
Document	237.1 (6.8)	259.9 (3.1)	292.1 (3.7)	301.4 (2.4)	329.9 (7.9)
Quantitative	241.3 (5.7)	264.9 (3.0)	298.7 (2.1)	311.2 (3.3)	346.8 (8.0)
Black					
Prose	206.3 (7.4)	244.0 (6.9)	273.4 (6.9)	286.7 (7.9)	306.5 (11.0)
Document	217.5 (15.0)	228.4 (5.4)	256.5 (3.5)	274.7 (5.6)	288.7 (6.9)
Quantitative	217.3 (19.6)	234.8 (4.0)	263.0 (4.3)	275.1 (7.7)	307.8 (9.2)
Hispanic					
Prose	203.4 (13.1)	229.2 (11.6)	278.3 (11.7)	277.8 (7.0)	304.7 (52.1)
Document	199.3 (14.0)	228.1 (10.5)	258.9 (10.8)	273.7 (8.9)	271.0 (22.9)
Quantitative	201.7 (11.2)	223.6 (8.1)	272.7 (9.9)	277.7 (10.9)	282.4 (35.1)

ES/UI Level of Education

Race/Ethnicity	0-8 Yrs.	9-12 Yrs.	H.S. Diploma or GED	Some Post-secondary	College Degree
White					
Prose	224.3 (8.1)	272.9 (4.2)	300.4 (2.3)	317.9 (2.6)	344.8 (4.1)
Document	225.0 (8.1)	269.6 (2.5)	293.7 (2.1)	309.2 (2.2)	326.9 (5.7)
Quantitative	238.2 (9.7)	271.7 (3.6)	301.7 (2.6)	313.8 (3.1)	336.0 (3.7)
Black					
Prose	201.4 (21.5)	230.5 (10.8)	256.6 (7.0)	283.1 (6.2)	290.1 (12.1)
Document	160.2 (12.3)	222.9 (12.7)	248.0 (4.4)	266.8 (6.3)	278.5 (17.8)
Quantitative	196.0 (21.8)	227.7 (12.4)	259.3 (7.7)	268.5 (4.5)	284.3 (13.5)
Hispanic					
Prose	176.2 (7.3)	227.5 (8.5)	261.2 (6.6)	275.0 (8.8)	274.4 (7.2)
Document	179.2 (14.0)	228.3 (5.2)	250.9 (5.8)	273.7 (6.3)	267.1 (11.3)
Quantitative	194.3 (9.3)	235.7 (6.2)	260.5 (4.5)	274.7 (7.1)	284.2 (6.4)

*The numbers in parentheses are estimated standard errors.

Alternative High School Certification

JTPA and ES/UI program participants who did not receive a high school diploma were asked whether or not they ever participated in a GED or high school equivalency program. Among ES/UI participants, about 46 percent indicate they had studied for the GED as compared with about 56 percent of eligible JTPA applicants (Table 4.6 in Section 4). More importantly, on each of three scales, those who report studying for the GED score about one-half of a standard deviation (or 25 points) higher than those who report not studying for the certificate.

Thus, among JTPA and ES/UI program participants without a high school diploma, those demonstrating higher levels of literacy are more likely to pursue the GED than those with lower levels of skill. At the time of this DOL assessment, some 60 percent of JTPA and ES/UI program participants who report studying for the GED also indicate receiving a certificate. Again, mean performance on the three literacy measures appears to be strongly related to whether or not a GED certificate was obtained. The differences in means shown in Table 3.6 of those who received the GED and those who did not range from 35 to 50 points on the three literacy scales. For example, the average prose score was 295 for JTPA eligible applicants who report receiving their GED and 247 for those who said they did not receive the certificate. Similarly, among ES/UI participants the prose scores were 291 as compared with 240. Whether these differences result primarily from learning gains that occur as a result of participation in the various programs or reflect pre-existing conditions, it appears that a GED certificate is a good proxy for higher literacy levels — that is, for both population groups, the mean literacy proficiency scores of those individuals receiving a GED are similar to those reporting a high school diploma.

Table 3.6	Weighted Average Proficiency Scores on the Three Literacy Scales for Those Who Study for the GED and Those Who Received the GED*			
	Study		Received	
	Yes	No	Yes	No
JTPA				
Prose	274.6 (4.6)	250.3 (5.6)	294.8 (4.1)	246.8 (7.7)
Document	270.5 (4.8)	244.3 (4.6)	285.4 (4.4)	250.1 (6.7)
Quantitative	273.1 (5.4)	249.5 (4.0)	289.1 (4.7)	251.1 (6.6)
ES/UI				
Prose	270.3 (6.2)	247.8 (8.5)	291.2 (6.0)	239.8 (8.2)
Document	268.3 (5.1)	240.8 (8.4)	284.7 (3.1)	244.6 (9.1)
Quantitative	276.6 (5.0)	248.8 (8.2)	293.3 (3.4)	254.7 (10.6)

*The numbers in parentheses are estimated standard errors.

During the past decade there have been a number of reports —
America's Choice: High Skills or Low Wages[4]; *Toward a More Perfect Union*[5]; *The Subtle
Danger*[6]; *Workplace Competencies: The Need to Improve Literacy and Employment
Readiness*[7]; *and Workforce 2000*[8]— that emphasize the role education and literacy play
in meeting the human resource needs of this country. In the DOL assessment,
individuals were asked a series of questions that relate to what they were doing the
week before taking the assessment, the number of weeks worked in the preceding 12
months, the type of job they held most recently, and their hourly wage in that job.
Analyses of the data in Tables 3.7 to 3.10 reveal that individuals who demonstrate
higher levels of literacy skills avoid long periods of unemployment, earn higher wages,
and work in higher level occupations as compared with those program participants
who demonstrate lower literacy skills.

Weeks of Employment and Labor Force Status

The pattern of results for the two DOL populations is very similar (Table 3.7).
That is, individuals who report longer periods of employment during the 12 months
preceding the survey demonstrate higher levels of proficiency than their counterparts
who report fewer weeks of employment. For example, JTPA eligible applicants who
report 13 or fewer weeks of employment achieve mean literacy scores of 276 or lower
on the three scales, while the mean scores for those reporting 27 or more weeks of
employment approximate the 290 level.

---

[4] National Center on Education. (1990). *America's choice: High skills or low wages.* The report of the
commission on the skills of the American workforce. (Rochester, NY: National Center on Education.)
[5] G. Berlin and A. Sum. (1988). *Toward a more perfect union: Basic skills, poor families, and our economic
future.* (Occasional paper 3) (New York: Ford Foundation.)
[6] R. L. Venezky, C. F. Kaestle, and A. M. Sum. (1987). *The subtle danger: Reflections on the literacy abilities
of America's young adults.* (Princeton, NJ: Educational Testing Service.)
[7] P. E. Barton and I. S. Kirsch. (1990). *Workplace competencies: The need to improve literacy and employment
readiness.* Policy perspectives series from Information Services within the Office of Educational Research
and Improvement. (Washington, DC: U.S. Department of Education.)
[8] Hudson Institute. (1987). *Workforce 2000: Work and workers for the 21st century.* (Indianapolis: Hudson
Institute, Inc., Herman Kahn Center.)

Table 3.7 Weighted Average Proficiency Scores on the Three Literacy Scales by Population, Labor Force Status, and Weeks of Employment*

*The numbers in parentheses are estimated standard errors.

The labor force status variable that characterizes the work pattern during the week preceding the assessment reveals the same pattern of results as does the variable of weeks of employment. Individuals in each of the DOL populations who report being employed the week prior to the assessment have average literacy scores at or above 290, while those who report being out of work and not looking for a job attain average proficiency scores of about 275 or below.

Earnings and Income

The data reported in Table 3.8 represent hourly wage information for those individuals in each population who report being employed the week prior to the assessment. This represents roughly 20 percent of the JTPA eligible applicants and nearly 40 percent of the ES/UI program participants. While the progression of mean proficiency scores is not as consistent as those discussed above, Table 3.8 reinforces the notion that hourly wages can be expected to increase in association with higher literacy proficiencies. For example, ES/UI participants who report earning between $3.86 and $4.99 attain average proficiencies between 265 and 275, while those who report earning $10.00 or more per hour demonstrate proficiencies at about the 315 level.

Table 3.8	Weighted Average Proficiency Scores on the Three Literacy Scales by Population and Hourly Wage*				
	n	Weighted N	Prose	Document	Quantitative
JTPA					
Up to $3.85	151	60,855	284.2 (8.1)	271.8 (7.6)	275.3 (6.7)
$3.86-$4.99	128	59,440	292.1 (6.9)	288.5 (7.7)	291.6 (7.3)
$5.00-$6.99	121	58,724	290.7 (11.0)	275.9 (7.7)	284.3 (9.3)
$7.00-$9.99	37	23,921	334.0 (22.4)	303.1 (22.1)	320.3 (14.9)
$10.00 +	38	29,271	321.3 (16.2)	293.5 (7.8)	298.8 (10.2)
ES/UI					
Up to $3.85	132	479,565	283.2 (7.5)	275.2 (7.3)	283.3 (8.6)
$3.86-$4.99	210	950,315	265.9 (6.1)	264.5 (7.4)	274.8 (6.4)
$5.00-$6.99	325	1,638,240	286.2 (4.1)	280.2 (4.3)	286.1 (3.5)
$7.00-$9.99	315	1,855,104	298.0 (3.3)	291.0 (4.9)	299.8 (3.0)
$10.00 +	289	2,114,811	314.2 (5.1)	313.3 (3.6)	318.7 (6.0)

*The numbers in parentheses are estimated standard errors.

A more consistent pattern emerges in the data displayed in Table 3.9 reflecting reported household income. As is typical with income and performance data, the range in mean proficiency scores is relatively wide across each of the DOL populations. This range in mean proficiency scores extends over a full standard deviation (in fact, some 60 points) for the ES/UI population and approaches a full standard deviation on the prose and quantitative scales for the JTPA eligible applicants.

| Table 3.9 | Weighted Average Proficiency Scores on the Three Literacy Scales by Population and Household Income* |

	n	Weighted N	Prose	Document	Quantitative
JTPA					
Up to $4,999	735	277,211	271.4 (3.8)	260.9 (2.6)	263.2 (3.7)
$5,000-9,999	594	245,040	286.2 (4.6)	280.0 (4.1)	285.1 (4.0)
$10,000-14,999	332	137,462	281.8 (4.7)	273.2 (3.8)	281.5 (5.5)
$15,000-19,999	175	83,094	297.4 (10.4)	292.9 (6.2)	291.9 (5.7)
$20,000-29,999	188	107,308	296.5 (6.0)	289.8 (4.1)	297.5 (5.9)
$30,000-39,999	121	70,315	314.1 (10.5)	294.3 (9.0)	309.3 (10.9)
$40,000-49,999	64	28,411	307.3 (10.4)	294.9 (7.3)	303.5 (9.1)
$50,000 +	28	19,464	315.8 (13.2)	287.4 (10.0)	305.5 (11.1)
ES/UI					
Up to $4,999	253	1,495,024	263.0 (6.4)	257.2 (6.1)	265.8 (5.3)
$5,000-9,999	359	2,059,540	267.8 (6.8)	261.4 (6.7)	270.8 (6.4)
$10,000-14,999	423	2,362,704	281.5 (6.2)	268.2 (6.0)	278.5 (4.0)
$15,000-19,999	357	1,917,485	286.2 (8.0)	277.0 (5.9)	287.1 (5.6)
$20,000-29,999	585	3,009,634	293.4 (5.3)	290.4 (3.9)	296.4 (5.6)
$30,000-39,999	428	2,437,458	309.5 (4.2)	302.1 (2.5)	304.0 (4.3)
$40,000-49,999	273	1,478,380	305.3 (3.5)	296.7 (3.4)	303.8 (3.7)
$50,000 +	328	2,270,563	324.0 (4.4)	320.5 (2.5)	325.3 (5.3)

*The numbers in parentheses are estimated standard errors.

Occupations

While it would be beneficial to know the level of literacy required to find employment and succeed in various occupations, there is no research available that allows such statements to be made with any confidence. Still, some perspective can be gained by looking at the demonstrated proficiency levels of people in the DOL populations who report having worked in various occupational categories.

The data in Table 3.10 indicate that the literacy levels of individuals reporting various occupations do differ considerably. In fact, the range of mean proficiency scores for both DOL populations extends over almost a full standard deviation (50 points) on each of the three scales. For example, individuals who report working in professional positions have average prose and quantitative proficiencies around the 320 level compared with those who report working in laborer and service occupations, where the means are around the 270 level. On the document scale, the means range from about 300 for those reporting professional occupations to about 265 for those reporting laborer and service occupations.

	n	Weighted N	Prose	Document	Quantitative
JTPA					
Laborer	258	123,678	272.2 (3.8)	264.8 (4.7)	268.0 (4.6)
Service	543	234,016	276.9 (4.6)	265.9 (4.3)	274.1 (4.8)
Operative	417	200,639	282.8 (4.3)	274.4 (3.9)	281.1 (4.4)
Craft	206	92,762	280.2 (6.1)	280.3 (6.7)	284.9 (7.5)
Clerical	228	96,811	304.8 (5.3)	288.4 (5.7)	297.3 (5.2)
Sales	287	115,263	298.8 (5.7)	286.6 (6.3)	291.7 (5.2)
Technical	31	13,103	316.4 (18.7)	303.5 (12.8)	303.9 (8.6)
Manager	111	54,675	313.9 (8.1)	298.3 (7.0)	314.6 (6.8)
Professional	70	38,656	319.5 (19.1)	299.5 (14.3)	317.7 (15.4)
ES/UI					
Laborer	311	1,573,455	268.5 (10.3)	268.4 (9.5)	273.9 (9.2)
Service	411	2,076,633	274.0 (6.1)	262.3 (6.4)	274.1 (6.2)
Operative	554	3,074,901	270.9 (6.2)	264.5 (4.7)	274.2 (5.1)
Craft	379	2,100,824	285.5 (4.8)	283.2 (4.0)	290.4 (3.6)
Clerical	430	2,751,452	296.5 (5.7)	284.8 (4.3)	289.6 (4.3)
Sales	396	2,325,324	301.6 (5.0)	296.4 (4.3)	303.2 (3.7)
Technical	74	371,848	315.8 (10.5)	307.1 (13.0)	306.4 (11.5)
Manager	389	2,546,878	319.5 (5.1)	312.7 (3.0)	318.1 (3.4)
Professional	178	1,101,416	322.4 (6.2)	312.1 (5.0)	323.2 (6.4)

*The numbers in parentheses are estimated standard errors.

While the range of average proficiency scores is similar in each DOL population, the grouping of the occupations is somewhat different. That is, for the eligible JTPA applicants two clusters seem to emerge. Those individuals who report laborer, service, operative, or craft occupations demonstrate literacy proficiencies that cluster around 270 to 280. In contrast, those reporting clerical through professional occupations have means that range from 290 to 320 on the literacy scales.

Within the ES/UI population, three clusters of occupational groups emerge. The average proficiency scores for individuals reporting laborer, service, or operative occupations center around the 270 level. For craft and clerical occupations, the means approximate 290 and for sales through professional occupations, the means tend to exceed the 300 level.

Proficiency and Perceived Adequacy of Literacy Skills

As shown in Table 3.11, there are significant differences in literacy proficiency levels between those who report their reading, writing, and mathematics skills were adequate for their most recent job and those who report they were not. Without exception, those who report that their skills were adequate score significantly higher on the three scales than those who report that their skills were not adequate. The difference between these two groups is more than a standard deviation (about 50 points on a scale ranging from 0 to 500) for the prose and document scales and is somewhat smaller, about 80 percent of a standard deviation (40 points) for the quantitative scale. With respect to writing skills, the difference is at least two-thirds of a standard deviation (33 points) for all three scales, and for mathematics the difference is about half a standard deviation (25 points).

Table 3.11	Literacy Proficiency Levels for JTPA Applicants Reporting Adequacy of Literacy Skills for Their Most Recent Job*					
	Reading		Writing		Mathematics	
	Yes	No	Yes	No	Yes	No
Prose	289.6 (2.9)	223.9 (12.0)	290.2 (2.7)	251.1 (9.0)	289.7 (2.6)	265.1 (9.8)
Document	279.2 (3.0)	222.1 (10.0)	280.0 (3.0)	243.1 (7.2)	279.2 (2.9)	255.3 (7.9)
Quantitative	286.0 (2.9)	244.5 (14.1)	287.1 (2.8)	253.1 (9.1)	286.9 (3.0)	259.6 (9.8)

*The numbers in parentheses are estimated standard errors.

Table 3.12 shows the literacy proficiency levels by scale for each skill area for the ES/UI population. As with the JTPA population, those ES/UI participants who report that their skills were adequate score significantly higher on the literacy scales than those who report that their skills were not adequate. Across all three scales, the difference between the two groups is more than a standard deviation with respect to reading skills, is about two-thirds of a standard deviation for writing, and approaches or reaches 80 percent of a standard deviation for mathematics.

Table 3.12	Literacy Proficiency Levels for ES/UI Participants Reporting Adequacy of Literacy Skills for Their Most Recent Job*					
	Reading		Writing		Mathematics	
	Yes	No	Yes	No	Yes	No
Prose	294.8 (3.5)	226.3 (13.6)	295.1 (3.6)	261.6 (12.2)	294.8 (3.4)	258.7 (12.2)
Document	287.3 (2.8)	228.2 (14.5)	288.1 (2.8)	253.7 (10.7)	287.9 (2.8)	248.5 (10.9)
Quantitative	294.4 (2.6)	242.0 (9.8)	295.4 (2.8)	261.7 (9.5)	295.6 (2.7)	253.3 (8.6)

*The numbers in parentheses are estimated standard errors.

For the two DOL populations, no significant difference in mean score performance is demonstrated on the prose scale, but on the document and quantitative scales the means for the ES/UI population are significantly higher than those for eligible JTPA applicants. For the most part, there are no significant differences in mean scores between men and women in either DOL group. As revealed in these data, JTPA is serving a higher proportion of younger individuals (16 to 20 years of age), while ES/UI is serving a higher proportion of adults 46 years of age and older. Both DOL programs appear to be serving a less skilled subgroup of Hispanic participants than would be expected of a nationally representative total population sample, but there is evidence of a relatively strong self-selection factor operating in the other direction for eligible Black applicants for JTPA — JTPA programs seem to be attracting a more highly skilled subgroup of Black participants than would be expected in relation to a nationally representative population.

Except for individuals reporting zero to eight years of education, there are no significant differences in the mean literacy proficiencies between the two DOL populations reporting various levels of educational attainment. There is, however, an increase of mean proficiency scores across scales for each population as educational attainment increases. This strong relationship between level of education and literacy proficiency holds for each racial/ethnic subgroup within both the JTPA and ES/UI populations. Few significant differences are evidenced between the mean proficiency scores for JTPA and ES/UI racial/ethnic subgroups. Those JTPA and ES/UI participants who do not hold a high school diploma but who report studying for the GED typically score about one-half standard deviation (or 25 points) above those who report not pursuing the GED. But those individuals who study for and earn the GED, on average, score some 35 to 50 points (or up to a full standard deviation) higher than those who drop out of the GED program.

The data on employment history, earnings, and occupation indicate that individuals who avoid long periods of unemployment, earn higher wages, and work in higher-level jobs also demonstrate higher levels of literacy proficiency. On average, individuals who are characterized as out of the labor force — that is, report being out of work and not seeking employment — obtain lower mean literacy proficiencies than do individuals who report having been employed the week before participating in this assessment.

CHARACTERIZING
EDUCATIONAL
EXPERIENCES OF
JTPA AND ES/UI
POPULATIONS

Because of the strong relationship between educational attainment and literacy proficiencies, this section characterizes the DOL populations in terms of several variables relating to their educational experiences. Given that all but a small percentage of the DOL client groups report at least some high school, experiences associated with this level of education are highlighted here. Specifically, these variables are:

- literacy materials in the home while in high school;

- work experience while in high school;

- highest grade of school completed;

- reasons for not completing high school; and,

- studying for and receiving the GED.

A useful framework for examining these educationally related variables includes: race/ethnicity, level of education, age, and labor force status. The race/ethnicity data are reported for the White, Black, and Hispanic subpopulations. The five categories of educational level include zero to eight years, nine to 12 years but no high school diploma, a high school diploma or general educational development certificate (GED), some postsecondary education, and a two- or four-year degree or higher. Age data are categorized into 16 to 20, 21 to 25, 26 to 31, 32 to 45, and 46 or older. Labor force status characterizes the work pattern during the week preceding the assessment: employed, not employed and looking for work, and out of the labor force — that is, out of work and not looking for a job. The tables in this section highlight various interesting patterns of relationships. More complete information on these variables can be found in Chapter 3 and in Appendix E of the Final Report.[1]

● LITERACY MATERIALS IN THE HOME

JTPA and ES/UI clients were asked if they had any of six different materials written in English in their home while in high school. The list included a daily or weekly newspaper, magazines, more than 25 books, an encyclopedia, a dictionary, and a personal computer. The data in Table 4.1 show that by and large, the two DOL client groups report comparable access to literacy materials in the home while growing up. Somewhat more than 70 percent of each group report the presence of printed materials in their homes while only 6 or 7 percent report access to a computer in the home.

Table 4.1	Percentages of JTPA and ES/UI Populations Reporting the Presence of Specific Literacy Materials in the Home While in High School*

	JTPA			ES/UI		
	Total n	Weighted N	In the Home	Total n	Weighted N	In the Home
Newspapers	2,484	1,084,264	84.1 (1.4)	3,263	18,866,194	85.6 (1.3)
Magazines	2,475	1,072,811	83.3 (1.3)	3,260	18,867,922	84.6 (1.3)
> 25 books	2,469	1,065,842	74.6 (1.5)	3,254	18,800,127	77.7 (2.0)
Encyclopedia	2,477	1,074,532	74.2 (1.3)	3,255	18,810,660	76.2 (1.1)
Dictionary	2,471	1,075,294	92.7 (0.7)	3,252	18,732,210	94.9 (0.8)
Personal Computer	2,434	1,039,718	6.2 (1.2)	3,199	18,505,078	7.5 (0.6)

*The numbers in parentheses are estimated standard errors.

While not shown here, the average number of materials listed are not different for each of the total DOL populations — the average is 4.1 materials among JTPA applicants and 4.2 among ES/UI participants. Moreover, when these averages are examined by race/ethnicity, level of education, age, and labor force status, no significant differences emerge. There is a tendency, however, for older individuals, those with the least amount of education, and Hispanic subgroups to report having had access to fewer listed materials.

---

[1] I. S. Kirsch and A. Jungeblut. (1992). *Profiling the literacy proficiencies of JTPA and ES/UI populations: Final report to the Department of Labor.* (Princeton, NJ: Educational Testing Service.)

● WORK EXPERIENCE WHILE IN HIGH SCHOOL

One area of particular concern to policymakers is the work experience of students while they are attending high school. To address this issue, JTPA eligible applicants and ES/UI participants were asked to indicate whether they worked more than 20 hours a week during high school. Although not shown here, some 63 percent of JTPA applicants and 59 percent of ES/UI participants report that they did not work more than 20 hours a week while in high school. Table 4.2 indicates the percentages of each population who report working year-round, summers only, and during the school year. By far the largest percentage of those who report working more than 20 hours a week indicate that they worked year-round — nearly twice the percentage report working all year as compared with the combined percentages for summer only and school year only.

As with the total populations, a larger percentage of each racial/ethnic subgroup report working year round than either summers only or school year only. However, a significantly smaller percentage of Black JTPA and ES/UI populations report working year round than do their White counterparts. On the other hand, a significantly higher percentage of Black and Hispanic ES/UI participants report working more than 20 hours a week during the school year than do White participants. A similar pattern emerged for the JTPA applicants but is not statistically significant for the Hispanic subgroup.

For both DOL populations, a smaller percentage of those individuals indicating nine to 12 years of education report working year-round as compared with those having a high school diploma or GED. Among the different age groups, an interesting pattern emerges — typically larger percentages of both JTPA and ES/UI younger client groups report working during the school year than is the case for those 46 years of age and older.

● HIGHEST GRADE OF SCHOOL COMPLETED

As shown in Table 4.3, nearly 45 percent of JTPA applicants and 35 percent of ES/UI participants report having earned a high school diploma or GED certificate. Slightly more than 20 percent of JTPA applicants report some postsecondary educational experience (17 percent) or a college degree (6 percent). In contrast, a significantly larger percentage of ES/UI participants report some postsecondary schooling (27 percent) or a college degree (19 percent).

There are no significant differences in educational attainment by racial/ethnic group among the JTPA population. In contrast, a significantly larger percentage of

	n	Weighted N	Yes Yr.-Round	Yes Summer Only	Yes School Yr.
Table 4.2 Percentages of JTPA Applicants and ES/UI Participants Who Report Working More Than 20 Hours a Week While in High School for All Year, Summer Only, and School Year Only*					
TOTAL JTPA	2,484	1,094,832	22.3 (1.6)	6.9 (1.5)	4.5 (0.7)
RACE/ETHNICITY					
White	1,550	758,701	24.9 (2.1)	7.2 (2.0)	3.2 (0.6)
Black	657	229,0/7	14.4 (3.1)	7.3 (1.8)	7.0 (1.6)
Hispanic	157	64,470	25.6 (7.8)	2.2 (1.6)	11.2 (4.1)
LEVEL OF EDUCATION					
9-12 Years	702	301,652	18.5 (2.0)	7.2 (1.9)	4.8 (1.3)
H.S. Dip. or GED	1,038	482,488	25.8 (2.4)	6.7 (1.6)	4.3 (0.9)
Some Postsecondary	439	183,665	25.2 (3.2)	7.6 (1.7)	6.6 (1.7)
College Degree	130	61,480	23.6 (6.2)	10.4 (5.9)	0.4 (0.3)
AGE					
16-20	485	184,590	21.4 (3.3)	6.1 (2.2)	5.8 (1.9)
21-25	482	212,221	23.3 (2.8)	8.6 (2.9)	4.0 (1.3)
26-31	502	232,856	19.9 (2.5)	5.9 (1.9)	5.0 (1.7)
32-45	728	339,546	24.1 (2.4)	6.4 (1.2)	4.7 (1.7)
46+	259	115,018	21.6 (3.8)	8.7 (3.2)	1.7 (1.2)
LABOR FORCE STATUS					
Employed	488	239,754	27.6 (2.8)	7.8 (2.5)	3.8 (0.9)
Not Employed	825	351,988	21.7 (2.9)	8.3 (2.2)	4.7 (1.1)
Out of Labor Force	1,171	503,090	20.2 (2.2)	5.5 (1.0)	4.6 (0.9)
TOTAL ES/UI	3,251	18,774,745	26.0 (1.3)	9.8 (1.1)	4.2 (0.7)
RACE/ETHNICITY					
White	2,381	11,843,615	29.0 (1.3)	10.4 (0.8)	2.9 (0.6)
Black	373	2,183,531	17.6 (2.9)	8.2 (2.4)	6.1 (1.3)
Hispanic	376	3,767,035	22.7 (4.7)	8.6 (1.7)	7.3 (1.4)
LEVEL OF EDUCATION					
9-12 Years	500	2,941,253	19.7 (3.8)	11.0 (2.2)	4.4 (1.1)
H.S. Dip. or GED	1,270	6,646,561	28.7 (2.1)	6.9 (0.9)	4.4 (0.8)
Some Postsecondary	854	5,092,539	30.4 (1.5)	9.9 (1.3)	5.4 (1.8)
College Degree	511	3,589,282	22.0 (1.9)	15.3 (1.8)	1.8 (0.8)
AGE					
16-20	314	1,845,836	28.2 (7.1)	10.3 (2.1)	9.5 (3.5)
21-25	609	3,385,089	31.0 (2.9)	6.6 (1.9)	6.8 (2.9)
26-31	720	4,116,183	32.9 (1.9)	9.8 (1.2)	3.1 (1.1)
32-45	1,051	6,045,728	22.5 (1.5)	10.4 (1.6)	3.2 (0.9)
46+	544	3,302,979	16.8 (1.5)	11.9 (2.0)	1.6 (0.5)
LABOR FORCE STATUS					
Employed	1,291	7,101,245	26.4 (2.2)	7.5 (1.0)	4.3 (1.5)
Not Employed	1,116	6,361,005	27.6 (1.3)	13.0 (1.6)	4.0 (0.9)
Out of Labor Force	844	5,312,494	23.5 (2.2)	9.0 (2.2)	4.1 (1.1)

*The numbers in parentheses are estimated standard errors.

	n	Weighted N	0-8 Yrs.	9-12 Yrs.	H.S. Dip. or GED	Some Postsec.	College Degree
TOTAL JTPA	2,498	1,097,953	5.9 (1.1)	27.5 (1.6)	44.1 (2.1)	16.8 (1.7)	5.6 (1.3)
RACE/ETHNICITY							
White	1,555	760,582	5.5 (1.3)	26.7 (2.1)	46.3 (2.3)	14.9 (1.5)	6.5 (1.7)
Black	662	229,460	6.0 (1.9)	29.9 (4.9)	40.3 (5.1)	20.8 (4.5)	3.0 (1.5)
Hispanic	159	64,912	8.1 (3.0)	22.1 (2.9)	38.5 (5.0)	24.6 (6.4)	6.6 (2.6)
AGE							
16-20	489	185,317	11.0 (2.9)	51.6 (5.2)	31.4 (3.5)	6.0 (1.9)	0.0 (0.0)
21-25	485	213,863	2.1 (0.6)	25.5 (2.4)	54.0 (3.2)	16.5 (2.6)	1.9 (0.8)
26-31	505	233,885	4.5 (1.2)	29.1 (3.1)	44.6 (4.1)	15.2 (3.6)	6.7 (2.8)
32-45	732	340,060	4.5 (1.5)	18.4 (3.3)	44.0 (3.8)	23.0 (2.9)	10.1 (2.3)
46+	258	114,073	8.8 (3.0)	15.0 (3.3)	49.0 (5.7)	20.5 (4.6)	6.6 (2.3)
LABOR FORCE STATUS							
Employed	492	241,746	3.5 (1.1)	24.3 (3.7)	45.8 (3.6)	16.9 (2.0)	9.5 (4.1)
Not Employed	828	352,886	4.5 (0.9)	21.3 (2.3)	46.6 (3.0)	20.2 (2.2)	7.4 (1.5)
Out of Labor Force	1,178	503,321	8.1 (1.6)	33.5 (2.7)	41.6 (2.4)	14.4 (2.2)	2.5 (0.7)
TOTAL ES/UI	3,273	18,890,282	2.7 (0.6)	15.6 (2.0)	35.4 (1.6)	27.3 (2.3)	19.1 (1.3)
RACE/ETHNICITY							
White	2,392	11,887,017	1.2 (0.3)	11.6 (1.4)	36.5 (2.0)	28.2 (2.9)	22.3 (1.9)
Black	375	2,189,197	0.6 (0.4)	18.4 (3.2)	45.1 (7.8)	27.0 (3.8)	8.9 (1.7)
Hispanic	383	3,809,344	8.0 (2.8)	28.0 (6.4)	28.5 (2.2)	25.9 (5.3)	9.6 (1.6)
AGE							
16-20	313	1,841,159	1.2 (1.1)	35.2 (6.5)	43.4 (5.0)	18.4 (2.7)	1.8 (1.5)
21-25	616	3,418,336	2.6 (1.5)	19.2 (2.9)	42.0 (4.5)	26.2 (2.6)	10.0 (2.0)
26-31	727	4,146,004	1.2 (0.5)	14.1 (2.3)	38.6 (3.0)	27.3 (2.0)	18.8 (1.8)
32-45	1,057	6,092,100	3.8 (0.7)	10.4 (1.6)	30.4 (1.7)	29.5 (2.9)	25.9 (2.4)
46+	546	3,308,221	3.7 (1.8)	10.8 (2.1)	29.7 (3.0)	29.7 (5.6)	26.2 (3.6)
LABOR FORCE STATUS							
Employed	1,298	7,149,839	2.2 (0.6)	11.1 (1.8)	36.3 (1.9)	31.7 (1.9)	18.7 (1.9)
Not Employed	1,125	6,402,645	2.4 (0.6)	16.1 (2.5)	35.5 (2.6)	24.3 (2.9)	21.8 (1.9)
Out of Labor Force	850	5,337,797	3.7 (1.0)	21.0 (2.8)	34.0 (2.5)	25.0 (3.4)	16.3 (1.7)

Table 4.3 Highest Grade of School Completed for JTPA Applicants and ES/UI Participants by Race/Ethnicity, Age, and Labor Force Status*

*The numbers in parentheses are estimated standard errors.

White ES/UI participants report having a college degree than do either Black or Hispanic ES/UI participants. Furthermore, when compared with either Black or White ES/UI participants, a larger percentage of Hispanic respondents report zero to eight years of schooling while a significantly smaller percentage report earning a high school diploma or GED.

A significantly larger percentage of JTPA applicants aged 16 to 20 report zero to eight years of education than do applicants in the three age ranges from 21 through 45. With respect to labor force status, a significantly higher percentage of eligible applicants not employed but looking for a job, and thus still in the labor force, report earning a college degree than do those individuals classified as out of the labor force. In addition, significantly higher percentages of JTPA applicants who did not earn a high school diploma or GED report being out of the work force. While a few comparisons are statistically significant, there do not appear to be any meaningful trends in the age or employment status variables for the ES/UI participants.

● REASONS GIVEN FOR NOT COMPLETING HIGH SCHOOL

Since educational attainment is among the best predictors of literacy proficiencies, it is of particular interest to understand better some of the experiences of JTPA applicants and ES/UI participants who report not earning a high school diploma. As shown in the Final Report, some 42 percent of JTPA and 23 percent of ES/UI client groups report leaving school before earning a high school diploma. These individuals were asked why they stopped their schooling when they did. Responses to this open-ended question were categorized into one of the following: financial problems, going to work or into the military, pregnancy, loss of interest in school and/or behavior problems, poor grades or academic problems, family or personal problems that were not necessarily school related, and other.

Table 4.4 shows the distributions of reasons given by JTPA applicants for not completing high school. The two most frequently reported reasons for dropping out of school are family problems and lack of interest in school. This is true for White and Hispanic applicants; however, for Black applicants, the main reasons given are family problems and pregnancy. Across the variables of interest reported here, relatively few JTPA applicants cite academic problems as the primary reason for not completing high school. The same finding was noted in the 1986 young adult literacy assessment.

| | | | Table 4.4 | Reason Reported by JTPA Applicants for Dropping Out of School by Race/Ethnicity, Age, and Labor Force Status* | | | | |

	n	Weighted N	Financial Problem	Working/ Military	Pregnant	No Interest	Academic Problem	Family Problem
TOTAL	1,058	429,238	2.6 (0.9)	15.7 (1.9)	13.8 (1.7)	20.0 (1.6)	5.7 (0.8)	23.1 (2.0)**
RACE/ETHNICITY								
White	677	292,345	3.1 (1.1)	14.3 (1.7)	12.3 (1.9)	21.9 (2.2)	5.3 (1.2)	22.5 (2.0)
Black	251	87,240	0.7 (0.2)	14.2 (4.0)	20.5 (3.3)	16.9 (3.2)	5.3 (1.1)	26.0 (4.7)
Hispanic	66	22,929	3.7 (3.0)	14.5 (3.3)	12.8 (8.6)	15.5 (2.6)	9.0 (4.5)	27.5 (7.6)
AGE								
16-20	304	112,984	2.3 (1.3)	10.0 (3.1)	12.0 (2.7)	24.3 (4.0)	6.0 (1.4)	19.8 (3.5)
21-25	180	68,498	2.3 (2.1)	12.2 (3.7)	16.0 (4.0)	30.1 (5.6)	2.9 (1.1)	21.8 (4.4)
26-31	211	94,143	0.3 (0.3)	19.6 (4.4)	14.8 (4.1)	16.7 (3.0)	3.5 (0.9)	26.2 (3.3)
32-45	248	106,125	5.3 (2.1)	18.1 (4.0)	14.2 (3.3)	15.7 (4.5)	8.2 (2.9)	22.1 (4.3)
46+	98	40,329	3.0 (1.7)	21.4 (5.0)	8.6 (4.1)	10.7 (4.6)	8.8 (3.5)	34.1 (8.8)
LABOR FORCE STATUS								
Employed	187	83,891	1.7 (1.2)	15.4 (3.3)	11.8 (3.6)	19.6 (3.2)	3.5 (1.5)	17.6 (3.0)
Not Employed	308	118,001	4.7 (2.2)	31.6 (6.1)	3.3 (1.1)	20.9 (3.9)	6.3 (2.0)	20.7 (3.3)
Out of Labor Force	563	227,347	1.9 (0.9)	7.5 (1.7)	19.9 (3.6)	19.7 (2.4)	6.1 (1.0)	26.4 (2.8)

* The numbers in parentheses are estimated standard errors.
** Figures do not add up to 100 percent because the percentages for the "other" category are not included.

Yet the data in both assessments indicate a very strong relationship between literacy skills and academic achievement.

For all age groups, one of the two main reasons for not completing high school is family problems; however, for 16- to 20-year-olds and 21- to 25-year-olds, lack of interest is the other frequently cited reason, while for the other three age groups the other main reason is going to work or into the military. With respect to employment status, for those who were not employed, going to work or into the military is the most reported reason for leaving school, followed by lack of interest and family problems. For those out of the labor force, pregnancy is another significant reason for dropping out of high school.

Table 4.5 shows the distributions of reasons given by ES/UI participants for not completing high school. Across each of the variables of interest reported here, the two most salient reasons given for leaving school before earning a diploma are family problems and entering either the work force or the military. Lack of interest in schooling is also cited frequently. For Black ES/UI participants, pregnancy is cited about as frequently as going to work or into the military. As with the JTPA applicants, academic problems are not frequently given as the main reason for leaving school.

Table 4.5	Reason Reported by ES/UI Participants for Dropping Out of School by Race/Ethnicity, Age, and Labor Force Status*

	n	Weighted N	Financial Problem	Working/ Military	Pregnant	No Interest	Academic Problem	Family Problem
TOTAL	770	4,080,972	4.2 (1.4)	29.5 (2.7)	9.1 (1.2)	15.5 (2.4)	3.4 (0.9)	22.6 (2.6)**
RACE/ETHNICITY								
White	504	2,201,118	3.1 (1.0)	28.9 (2.6)	6.2 (2.2)	17.8 (2.1)	3.5 (1.1)	25.4 (3.7)
Black	95	474,346	0.6 (0.7)	29.3 (3.9)	24.9 (2.8)	17.2 (5.2)	5.1 (2.7)	15.1 (6.3)
Hispanic	149	1,258,229	7.5 (3.1)	33.9 (7.3)	7.9 (4.2)	7.7 (0.7)	1.7 (1.2)	21.1(11.3)
AGE								
16-20	100	568,019	9.1 (8.9)	20.6 (8.6)	2.0 (1.0)	17.7 (5.3)	4.1 (3.0)	20.7 (5.6)
21-25	139	915,980	3.7 (1.6)	35.1 (3.0)	7.9 (3.1)	16.4 (2.6)	1.5 (0.6)	20.4 (4.0)
26-31	158	808,675	2.0 (0.9)	29.4 (7.3)	14.8 (4.3)	20.3 (5.4)	4.6 (2.4)	14.9 (3.6)
32-45	232	1,154,193	2.3 (1.1)	23.7 (5.1)	11.1 (2.5)	14.0 (4.1)	4.8 (1.6)	31.3 (5.5)
46+	135	575,104	7.2 (2.7)	44.0 (4.3)	4.6 (2.0)	9.2 (2.5)	1.4 (1.0)	23.6 (4.3)
LABOR FORCE STATUS								
Employed	278	1,301,798	7.3 (4.2)	27.2 (5.5)	10.0 (1.4)	15.5 (3.6)	2.1 (0.9)	28.3 (2.8)
Not Employed	257	1,452,295	2.6 (0.9)	37.1 (4.5)	4.6 (1.8)	16.3 (2.5)	2.4 (0.7)	19.9 (5.1)
Out of Labor Force	235	1,326,878	2.8 (1.2)	23.4 (2.4)	13.1 (2.2)	14.5 (4.4)	5.7 (2.6)	19.8 (3.2)

* The numbers in parentheses are estimated standard errors.
** Figures do not add up to 100 percent because the percentages for the "other" category are not included.

• STUDYING FOR AND RECEIVING A GED

JTPA and ES/UI respondents who report not earning a high school diploma were also asked if they had ever studied for or received a GED. As shown in Table 4.6, 56 percent of eligible JTPA applicants who had not earned a high school diploma indicate that they had studied for the GED. This rate of participation generally is the same among racial/ethnic groups, although there is a slightly lower rate for Hispanic applicants than for Black applicants. As might be expected, a significantly lower percentage of those aged 16 to 20 had studied for the GED as compared with other age categories, but there seem to be no significant differences in participation rates among those who report being employed, unemployed, and out of the labor force.

Table 4.6 also shows that of the ES/UI participants who were asked if they had ever studied for a GED, just under half (46 percent) respond that they had. As with JTPA applicants, a smaller percentage of Hispanic ES/UI participants (34 percent) report studying for the GED compared with White (52 percent) and Black (52 percent) ES/UI participants. Although there is a tendency for fewer ES/UI participants aged 46 and older to report studying for a GED, this difference is not significant. There are no significant differences in the GED participation rates among those who report being employed, unemployed, or out of the labor force.

Table 4.6

Percentages of JTPA Applicants and ES/UI Participants Who Report Studying
for the GED by Race/Ethnicity, Age, and Labor Force Status*

	JTPA				ES/UI			
	n	Weighted N	Yes	No	n	Weighted N	Yes	No
TOTAL	843	337,500	55.9 (2.3)	44.1 (2.3)	692	3,694,534	45.9 (4.3)	54.1 (4.3)
RACE/ETHNICITY								
White	545	241,084	54.0 (2.8)	46.0 (2.8)	451	2,004,132	51.6 (4.1)	48.4 (4.1)
Black	191	54,650	59.1 (4.8)	40.9 (4.8)	89	479,037	51.7 (4.1)	48.3 (4.1)
Hispanic	59	19,768	46.2 (4.4)	53.8 (4.4)	132	1,075,716	34.2 (6.9)	65.8 (6.9)
AGE								
16-20	233	86,290	36.4 (6.5)	63.6 (6.5)	72	439,862	46.2 (7.0)	53.8 (7.0)
21-25	141	54,196	66.8 (7.8)	33.2 (7.8)	126	836,125	42.9 (9.8)	57.1 (9.8)
26-31	168	72,913	59.2 (7.6)	40.8 (7.6)	144	726,761	52.1 (8.2)	47.9 (8.2)
32-45	216	88,293	65.6 (5.6)	34.4 (5.6)	215	1,061,612	47.1 (7.1)	52.9 (7.1)
46+	77	32,174	57.1 (7.0)	42.9 (7.0)	128	565,640	38.3 (8.4)	61.7 (8.4)
LABOR FORCE STATUS								
Employed	151	71,503	49.7 (6.7)	50.3 (6.7)	250	1,219,207	50.2 (4.6)	49.8 (4.6)
Not Employed	270	105,107	61.4 (3.6)	38.6 (3.6)	233	1,353,068	50.5 (6.1)	49.5 (6.1)
Out of Labor Force	422	160,889	55.0 (3.9)	45.0 (3.9)	209	1,122,258	35.8 (5.9)	64.2 (5.9)

*The numbers in parentheses are estimated standard errors.

Perhaps more important than the question of who participates in GED programs is the question of who completes them. Table 4.7 shows the percentages of JTPA applicants and ES/UI participants who received a GED as well as those who did not receive a GED. Some 60 percent of those JTPA applicants who report having studied for the GED actually received it. There are no significant differences by racial/ethnic group membership or labor force status in the percentages of JTPA applicants who report receiving the GED. However, less than half of the Hispanic applicants who were asked about studying for the GED indicate they had, yet of those applicants who had studied, about 66 percent report they had received the GED. In addition, with one exception, there are no differences in the percentages of JTPA applicants in the different age categories who report receiving a GED certificate. As might be expected, a lower percentage of those aged 16 to 20 report receiving a GED than any other age group.

Table 4.7

Percentages of JTPA Applicants and ES/UI Participants Who Report Receiving a GED Certificate by Race/Ethnicity, Age, and Labor Force Status*

	JTPA				ES/UI			
	n	Weighted N	Yes	No	n	Weighted N	Yes	No
TOTAL	461	186,424	58.8 (4.9)	41.2 (4.9)	326	1,621,949	61.3 (4.5)	38.7 (4.5)
RACE/ETHNICITY								
White	296	130,773	60.9 (6.0)	39.1 (6.0)	237	1,022,587	70.2 (4.8)	29.8 (4.8)
Black	112	29,554	51.4 (6.1)	48.6 (6.1)	48	247,493	45.7 (12.0)	54.3 (12.0)
Hispanic	28	9,314	65.8 (8.7)	34.2 (8.7)	32	304,977	45.6 (12.4)	54.4 (12.4)
AGE								
16-20	68	30,722	37.8 (7.0)	62.2 (7.0)	26	189,859	27.9 (12.4)	72.1 (12.4)
21-25	92	36,910	54.6 (5.0)	45.4 (5.0)	60	333,215	61.6 (8.1)	38.4 (8.1)
26-31	116	43,252	56.9 (11.5)	43.1 (11.5)	85	379,858	70.5 (8.9)	29.5 (8.9)
32-45	136	55,668	66.8 (7.1)	33.2 (7.1)	108	485,338	66.5 (6.8)	33.5 (6.8)
46+	47	18,364	80.6 (6.4)	19.4 (6.4)	45	218,245	66.0 (11.7)	34.0 (11.7)
LABOR FORCE STATUS								
Employed	89	36,462	63.0 (7.3)	37.0 (7.3)	124	611,328	64.5 (8.8)	35.5 (8.8)
Not Employed	154	61,573	61.8 (7.0)	38.2 (7.0)	119	648,725	62.3 (5.7)	37.7 (5.7)
Out of Labor Force	218	88,390	54.9 (8.7)	45.1 (8.7)	83	361,897	54.3 (10.5)	45.7 (10.5)

*The numbers in parentheses are estimated standard errors.

As with the JTPA applicants, of those ES/UI participants who participated in a GED program, about 60 percent indicate they had received a GED certificate. In contrast with JTPA applicants, there are significant differences among the racial/ethnic groups: significantly lower percentages of Black and Hispanic ES/UI participants received a certificate as compared with White participants. With the exception of those aged 16 to 20, however, there are no differences by age in the percentages of ES/UI participants receiving a GED. Similarly, as with the JTPA applicants, there are no significant differences in the percentages receiving GED certificates among the different categories of labor force status. Among those studying for the GED, the difference in average proficiency scores is about 35 to 50 points, or a full standard deviation, in favor of those who attain the certificate over those who reported studying for the GED but not obtaining it. (It should be recalled that the proficiency scores associated with participation in a GED program and receiving the GED are discussed in Section 3 of this report and are shown by race/ethnicity and age in the Final Report.)

● SUMMARY

Of the education-related variables associated with the high school years, those referring to the number of literacy materials in the home and working more that 20 hours a week show no significant differences between the two DOL populations. Access to the printed materials listed is reported some seven times as frequently in each client group as is access to a computer while in high school. Nevertheless, there is a tendency for reported access to fewer literacy materials during the high school years among older individuals, those with the least amount of education, and Hispanic subgroup members. Although only about 40 percent of either the JTPA or ES/UI participants report working more than 20 hours a week while in high school, nearly twice the percentage in each group report working all year as compared with the combined percentages for summer only and school year only. Higher percentages of Black and Hispanic members of each population report working 20 or more hours during the school year than do White participants, but the difference is significant only for ES/UI groups. Similarly, larger percentages of younger DOL client groups report having worked 20 or more hours during high school than do individuals 46 years of age and older.

In terms of educational attainment, significantly larger percentages of ES/UI participants report some postsecondary training (27 percent) or a college degree or higher (19 percent) than do JTPA applicants — the percentages are 17 and 6, respectively. Some 58 and 77 percent of the JTPA and ES/UI participants report earning a high school diploma. Race/ethnicity is not a salient variable relating to educational attainment for JTPA applicants while, for ES/UI groups, smaller percentages of Black and Hispanic participants report attaining a college degree or higher than do White participants. Moreover, a larger percentage of Hispanic ES/UI participants report zero to eight years of schooling while a smaller percent report a high school diploma or GED than do their Black or White counterparts. Age and employment status appear to be important in relation to educational attainment for JTPA but not for ES/UI participants. Those JTPA applicants under the age of 21 and, over the age of 45 are most likely to report completing only zero to eight years of school; unemployed college graduates tend to be seeking a job rather than to be out of the labor force; and higher percentages of JTPA applicants who did not complete high school or the GED report being out of the work force.

Despite the strong association between educational attainment and demonstrated literacy proficiencies indicated in both the DOL and young adult data, only 10 percent or fewer of the ES/UI or JTPA participants report academic problems as the reason for not completing high school. The reasons that JTPA applicants report most frequently for dropping out of secondary school were family problems and lack of interest, whereas for ES/UI participants, entering the work force or the military and family problems lead the list — military service or entering the job market was, however, a very frequent reason reported by JTPA applicants over the age of 25. Pregnancy was also frequently cited by Black subgroup members of each DOL population and was also a salient reason for JTPA applicants who were out of the work force at the time of the assessment.

Roughly half of each DOL population report studying for the GED — 56 percent of JTPA applicants and 46 percent of ES/UI participants. The rate of participation among JTPA applicants is generally the same for racial/ethnic groups, age categories, and among those who report being employed, unemployed, or out of the labor force. Exceptions are that significantly smaller percentages of Hispanic applicants and JTPA applicants aged 16 to 20 report studying for the GED. A similar pattern of results is observed among ES/UI participants. While a smaller percentage of Hispanic ES/UI participants report studying for the GED when compared with White and Black subgroups, no significant differences are found among age categories or labor force status.

More importantly, perhaps, some 60 percent of each DOL population who report studying for the GED also indicate that they received the certificate. There is a significant difference (some 35 to 50 points) in the mean proficiency scores of those who attain the certificate compared with those who report studying for the GED but not obtaining it. In contrast with JTPA applicants where no significant differences were found among racial/ethnic groups, significantly smaller percentages of Black and Hispanic ES/UI participants received a certificate when compared with White participants.

SECTION 5

CHARACTERIZING ACTIVITIES AND PERCEPTIONS OF JTPA AND ES/UI POPULATIONS

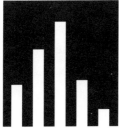

*I*t is widely held that literacy skills are important for full participation in our increasingly complex society with its formal institutions, complex legal system, and large government programs. In part, this belief is tied to research that shows literacy skills are related to various activities and practices. For this reason, respondents were asked several questions about activities that relate to their civic and political behaviors. One set of questions asked individuals about their current voter registration status and recent voting experiences. Another question focused on the frequency with which respondents keep abreast of government and public affairs.

Of further interest are the literacy activities respondents engage in both on the job and during their leisure time. JTPA and ES/UI populations were asked how often they read or used different types of materials at work — reports or journals, forms, letters, and diagrams or schematics. They were also asked how often they write or fill out business memos, letters, reports, forms, and bills or invoices. A final question asked how often they read a newspaper in English.

In addition to asking about current behaviors and activities, DOL client groups were also asked about their self-perceptions of their literacy skills. Specifically, they were asked to indicate whether or not they thought their reading, writing, and mathematics skills were good enough for their jobs. They were also questioned about whether they thought additional training would help them improve their job status. Finally, individuals were asked about the frequency with which others help them with various literacy activities.

As with the previous section of this report characterizing some of the educational experiences of these two DOL populations, the framework used here for examining activities and self-perceptions includes: race/ethnicity, level of education, age, and labor force status. The race/ethnicity data are reported for the White, Black, and Hispanic subpopulations. The five categories of educational level are: zero to eight years, nine to 12 years but no high school diploma, a high school diploma or general educational development certificate (GED), some postsecondary education, and a two- or four-year degree or higher. Age data are categorized into 16 to 20, 21 to 25, 26 to 31, 32 to 45, and 46 or older. Labor force status characterizes the work pattern during the week preceding the assessment: employed, not employed and looking for work, and out of the labor force — that is, out of work and not looking for a job. In some instances, the data are reported only for the total populations. Data Appendix E in the Final Report contains the complete distributions for the other variables.

● CIVIC EXPERIENCES

Voting Practices

Two survey questions asked respondents about their registration status and voting experiences. Table 5.1 shows the distributions of JTPA applicants who report being registered to vote and, of those, individuals who report ever voting in a public election. Of the 2,492 JTPA applicants who responded to this question, well over half (58 percent) indicate that they are currently registered to vote. There are no significant differences among the racial/ethnic subgroups with respect to being registered to vote.

Several factors seem to be related to whether or not a person participates in the voting process. Greater percentages of JTPA applicants with a high school diploma and above both registered to vote and voted as compared with those with some high school or less than high school. Among the three highest levels of education, however, the percentage of those with college degrees who voted is greater than the percentage of those with some postsecondary education, which, in turn, is greater than the percentage of those with a high school diploma or GED. Age also seems to be a factor. A significantly greater percentage of those over the age of 45 (79 percent) were registered as compared with those aged 32 to 45 (64 percent) and those between the ages of 21 and 31 (57 percent). Similarly, for those who are registered to vote, the likelihood of voting increases significantly by age. Ninety-two percent of those over age 45 report voting as compared with 81 percent of those aged 32 to 45, 64 percent of those aged 26 to 31, and 46 percent of those aged 21 to 25. There is also a relationship between participating in the voting process and employment status. Over half the applicants report being registered, regardless of employment status; over half of those registered, regardless of employment status, indicate that they had voted. A

Table 5.1	Distributions of JTPA Applicants with Respect to Voting Practices by Race/Ethnicity, Level of Education, Age, and Labor Force Status*							

	Currently Registered				Ever Voted			
	n	Weighted N	Yes	No	n	Weighted N	Yes	No
TOTAL	2,492	1,093,226	57.8 (2.7)	42.2 (2.7)	2,491	1,091,537	60.1 (3.0)	39.9 (3.0)
RACE/ETHNICITY								
White	1,550	757,194	56.4 (3.6)	43.6 (3.6)	1,551	756,185	61.3 (3.7)	38.7 (3.7)
Black	662	228,695	63.1 (4.1)	36.9 (4.1)	660	227,643	63.1 (3.7)	36.9 (3.7)
Hispanic	158	64,339	56.7 (6.1)	43.3 (6.1)	158	64,711	44.1 (6.5)	55.9 (6.5)
LEVEL OF EDUCATION								
0-8 Years	175	64,402	41.9 (6.1)	58.1 (6.1)	175	64,402	35.4 (6.5)	64.6 (6.5)
9-12 Years	704	302,056	45.8 (3.8)	54.2 (3.8)	703	300,487	43.2 (3.9)	56.8 (3.9)
H.S. Dip. or GED	1,041	480,383	60.1 (3.4)	39.9 (3.4)	1,040	480,358	62.5 (3.1)	37.5 (3.1)
Some Postsecondary	440	183,804	69.2 (2.6)	30.8 (2.6)	441	183,708	80.0 (2.0)	20.0 (2.0)
College Degree	130	61,480	80.7 (7.0)	19.3 (7.0)	130	61,480	90.0 (4.1)	10.0 (4.1)
AGE								
16-20	486	182,843	36.7 (4.5)	63.3 (4.5)	483	180,822	16.3 (2.8)	83.7 (2.8)
21-25	483	213,185	57.8 (4.1)	42.2 (4.1)	484	213,062	45.6 (2.9)	54.4 (2.9)
26-31	505	233,885	57.3 (3.7)	42.7 (3.7)	505	233,885	64.1 (3.7)	35.9 (3.7)
32-45	732	340,085	63.6 (3.1)	36.4 (3.1)	732	339,967	80.5 (2.4)	19.5 (2.4)
46+	257	112,475	78.7 (5.3)	21.3 (5.3)	258	113,047	91.7 (2.0)	8.3 (2.0)
LABOR FORCE STATUS								
Employed	492	241,746	61.3 (5.9)	38.7 (5.9)	491	240,945	63.3 (4.9)	36.7 (4.9)
Not Employed	826	351,792	63.5 (2.1)	36.5 (2.1)	828	352,793	65.3 (2.5)	34.7 (2.5)
Out of Labor Force	1,174	499,688	52.2 (2.9)	47.8 (2.9)	1,172	497,800	54.9 (4.3)	45.1 (4.3)

*The numbers in parentheses are estimated standard errors.

significantly lower percentage of those out of the labor force report being registered and voting, however, than those employed and those unemployed.

Table 5.2 shows that of the total ES/UI population, well over half (62 percent) report being registered, and 64 percent of those registered report that they had voted. Among the racial/ethnic populations, however, there are significant differences both for being registered and then for voting. Seventy-three percent of the Black participants report being registered as compared with 66 percent of the White participants and 46 percent of the Hispanic participants. Of those Hispanic participants registered, only 37 percent report having voted, as compared with 68 percent and 73 percent of the Black and White participants, respectively. Of the factors shown in Table 5.2, level of education and age seem to be related to both registering and then voting. The higher the level of education, the greater the percentages of those who were registered to vote and of those who voted. A significantly greater percentage of those over the age of 45 were registered as compared with the other age groups. Of those registered, however, those 46 and older (88 percent), those aged 32 to 45 (75 percent), and those aged 26 to 31 (63 percent) are more likely to vote than those in the 21- to 25-year-old age group (46 percent).

With respect to employment status, there are no significant differences among the three groups in their being registered to vote or having voted.

| Table 5.2 | Distributions of ES/UI Participants with Respect to Voting Practices by Race/Ethnicity, Level of Education, Age, and Labor Force Status* |

	Currently Registered				Ever Voted			
	n	Weighted N	Yes	No	n	Weighted N	Yes	No
TOTAL	3,271	18,876,238	62.1 (1.6)	37.9 (1.6)	3,266	18,822,927	63.6 (2.9)	36.4 (2.9)
RACE/ETHNICITY								
White	2,392	11,877,813	66.4 (2.0)	33.6 (2.0)	2,389	11,863,284	73.3 (2.2)	26.7 (2.2)
Black	375	2,189,197	73.2 (2.2)	26.8 (2.2)	375	2,189,197	67.5 (2.5)	32.5 (2.5)
Hispanic	381	3,804,504	46.1 (2.8)	53.9 (2.8)	381	3,771,409	37.0 (6.2)	63.0 (6.2)
LEVEL OF EDUCATION								
0-8 Years	119	509,013	28.6 (10.6)	71.4 (10.6)	119	509,013	32.5 (12.2)	67.5 (12.2)
9-12 Years	500	2,941,253	51.2 (1.8)	48.8 (1.8)	497	2,908,902	38.8 (3.5)	61.2 (3.5)
H.S. Dip. or GED	1,277	6,651,252	57.8 (2.4)	42.2 (2.4)	1,275	6,646,500	58.6 (2.1)	41.4 (2.1)
Some Postsecondary	859	5,150,723	67.6 (2.3)	32.4 (2.3)	860	5,153,143	72.8 (3.4)	27.2 (3.4)
College Degree	513	3,601,479	75.5 (2.2)	24.5 (2.2)	512	3,582,852	84.5 (2.3)	15.5 (2.3)
AGE								
16-20	314	1,845,836	41.5 (7.0)	58.5 (7.0)	311	1,813,484	19.4 (3.7)	80.6 (3.7)
21-25	614	3,414,423	60.1 (2.8)	39.9 (2.8)	615	3,416,843	45.9 (2.4)	54.1 (2.4)
26-31	725	4,128,849	58.4 (2.3)	41.6 (2.3)	725	4,142,468	62.7 (2.2)	37.3 (2.2)
32-45	1,058	6,094,447	63.6 (2.3)	36.4 (2.3)	1,058	6,105,371	74.9 (3.1)	25.1 (3.1)
46+	546	3,308,221	77.6 (2.8)	22.4 (2.8)	544	3,264,469	87.6 (2.0)	12.4 (2.0)
LABOR FORCE STATUS								
Employed	1,299	7,164,575	64.2 (1.7)	35.8 (1.7)	1,295	7,106,800	67.6 (3.4)	32.4 (3.4)
Not Employed	1,126	6,394,933	63.1 (1.9)	36.9 (1.9)	1,123	6,382,242	66.0 (2.8)	34.0 (2.8)
Out of Labor Force	846	5,316,729	58.0 (2.9)	42.0 (2.9)	848	5,333,885	55.3 (4.9)	44.7 (4.9)

*The numbers in parentheses are estimated standard errors.

Keeping Abreast of Public Affairs

One activity that is related to civic and political behavior is following government and public affairs. Table 5.3 shows the distributions of JTPA applicants who report following public affairs most of the time, some of the time, only now and then, or hardly at all. As can be seen from the table, over 70 percent of the total population report that they follow public affairs most or some of the time. This is also generally true for racial/ethnic groups. There does seem to be a relationship, however, between keeping up to date most of the time and both level of education and age. The higher one's education level, the more likely one is to follow current events. Greater percentages of those with a college degree or some postsecondary education report that they keep up to date most of the time as compared with those with a high school diploma or GED; in turn, a greater percentage of that group report that they follow public affairs as compared with those with less than a high school diploma or GED.

Also, as people get older, they tend to keep more up-to-date. The percentage of JTPA applicants who report keeping abreast of public affairs most of the time increases from 19 percent for those who are 16 to 20 years of age to just over 50 percent for those who are 46 years of age and older. While there is no difference between JTPA applicants who report being not employed and those out of the labor force, a significantly larger percentage of employed JTPA applicants report keeping abreast of public affairs most of the time than do those applicants who are out of the labor force. Since there are no significant differences among groups of JTPA applicants who follow public affairs some of the time, larger percentages of younger and/or less well-educated applicants report keeping abreast of public affairs only now and then or hardly at all.

Table 5.3	Distributions of JTPA Applicants and the Extent to Which They Report Keeping Abreast of Public Affairs by Race/Ethnicity, Level of Education, Age, and Labor Force Status*

	n	Weighted N	Most of the Time	Some of the Time	Only Now and Then	Hardly at All
TOTAL	2,496	1,094,391	35.5 (1.4)	37.2 (1.3)	16.1 (1.0)	11.1 (1.3)
RACE/ETHNICITY						
White	1,555	758,769	35.7 (2.0)	37.5 (1.3)	15.5 (1.4)	11.4 (1.5)
Black	660	227,711	34.2 (1.3)	37.3 (3.8)	18.2 (3.5)	10.4 (1.7)
Hispanic	159	64,912	39.7 (5.3)	29.0 (5.6)	19.0 (3.4)	12.3 (3.2)
LEVEL OF EDUCATION						
0-8 Years	176	64,975	26.6 (6.5)	31.1 (4.6)	23.9 (6.8)	18.3 (3.5)
9-12 Years	705	302,247	23.4 (3.2)	39.9 (4.0)	19.0 (2.2)	17.7 (2.9)
H.S. Dip. or GED	1,042	480,879	37.8 (2.5)	37.4 (2.3)	15.5 (1.7)	9.3 (1.9)
Some Postsecondary	441	183,708	46.5 (3.6)	33.6 (4.2)	13.8 (2.8)	6.1 (2.1)
College Degree	130	61,480	51.9 (4.7)	40.5 (5.9)	6.3 (2.8)	1.2 (1.1)
AGE						
16-20	488	183,607	19.0 (4.8)	40.0 (3.7)	21.8 (2.5)	19.2 (3.3)
21-25	484	213,062	28.5 (3.6)	38.4 (2.6)	18.3 (2.7)	14.7 (3.1)
26-31	504	233,703	36.2 (2.7)	36.2 (4.7)	16.7 (2.6)	10.8 (3.0)
32-45	733	340,218	43.4 (2.0)	36.7 (2.1)	13.7 (1.6)	6.2 (0.8)
46+	258	113,047	52.7 (4.3)	32.6 (4.6)	8.5 (2.4)	6.1 (2.1)
LABOR FORCE STATUS						
Employed	491	240,945	42.2 (3.0)	34.7 (2.6)	14.5 (1.6)	8.6 (1.9)
Not Employed	829	353,043	36.4 (2.7)	39.4 (2.6)	14.9 (1.9)	9.2 (1.8)
Out of Labor Force	1,176	500,403	31.6 (2.4)	36.9 (2.1)	17.8 (1.0)	13.7 (2.3)

*The numbers in parentheses are estimated standard errors.

Table 5.4 shows similar distributions of the answers of ES/UI program participants to the same question about following public affairs. As with the JTPA population, over 70 percent of the total ES/UI population report following public affairs most or some of the time. With the ES/UI population, race/ethnicity, level of education, and age seem to be associated with keeping abreast of public affairs most of the time. About 48 percent of the White participants report keeping up-to-date most of the time; however, the rate is about 36 percent for Black participants and 34 percent for Hispanic participants. While the difference between White and Black participants is statistically significant, the differences between Hispanic participants and White and Black participants are not statistically significant. As with the JTPA population, the higher the level of education and the older the respondent, the greater the percentages of those who report keeping abreast of public affairs frequently.

Table 5.4	Distributions of ES/UI Participants and the Extent to Which They Report Keeping Abreast of Public Affairs by Race/Ethnicity, Level of Education, Age, and Labor Force Status*

	n	Weighted N	Most of the Time	Some of the Time	Only Now and Then	Hardly at All
TOTAL	3,274	18,895,813	44.2 (2.1)	32.9 (1.0)	14.2 (1.2)	8.7 (1.4)
RACE/ETHNICITY						
White	2,393	11,893,307	48.3 (1.7)	32.0 (1.3)	13.6 (1.9)	6.0 (0.5)
Black	375	2,189,197	36.3 (4.5)	38.4 (2.2)	15.8 (1.2)	9.4 (4.0)
Hispanic	384	3,824,079	33.9 (8.9)	35.6 (5.0)	14.7 (1.3)	15.8 (4.9)
LEVEL OF EDUCATION						
0-8 Years	120	511,432	26.5 (5.0)	25.7 (5.6)	20.8 (6.3)	27.0 (3.7)
9-12 Years	500	2,941,253	26.1 (1.9)	35.8 (2.3)	21.9 (2.8)	16.2 (2.7)
H.S. Dip. or GED	1,279	6,681,481	38.7 (2.5)	37.5 (1.7)	13.2 (2.1)	10.6 (1.8)
Some Postsecondary	860	5,153,143	48.7 (2.6)	31.9 (2.2)	14.7 (1.3)	4.8 (0.7)
College Degree	512	3,585,985	65.1 (2.6)	24.7 (1.7)	8.0 (1.7)	2.1 (1.2)
AGE						
16-20	314	1,845,836	27.9 (4.3)	34.4 (5.4)	22.8 (2.7)	14.9 (2.6)
21-25	615	3,416,843	30.5 (3.0)	41.5 (2.0)	16.9 (1.5)	11.1 (2.6)
26-31	727	4,146,004	40.8 (3.1)	32.5 (2.6)	15.9 (2.0)	10.7 (1.6)
32-45	1,059	6,109,941	45.6 (2.4)	33.3 (1.7)	13.6 (2.1)	7.5 (1.4)
46+	545	3,292,727	68.9 (2.8)	22.9 (2.1)	5.6 (1.3)	2.6 (1.2)
LABOR FORCE STATUS						
Employed	1,299	7,164,575	44.4 (2.4)	34.3 (2.3)	14.2 (1.8)	7.1 (1.0)
Not Employed	1,127	6,410,428	44.8 (3.8)	30.6 (2.0)	14.4 (2.5)	10.2 (3.0)
Out of Labor Force	848	5,320,810	43.2 (3.1)	33.9 (3.1)	13.9 (1.7)	9.1 (1.9)

*The numbers in parentheses are estimated standard errors.

The percentages increase from about 26 for those who report less than a high school diploma or GED to 65 percent for those with a college degree. It is interesting to note, however, that in contrast to JTPA, a greater percentage of those with a college degree keep abreast of public affairs most of the time as compared with those with some postsecondary education. By age categories, the percentages increase from about 28 for 16- to 20-year-old participants to nearly 70 for those 46 years of age and older. Among ES/UI participants, employment status does not seem to be related to keeping abreast of public affairs.

• CURRENT LITERACY ACTIVITIES

Reading Activities on the Job

The literacy activities respondents engage in both on the job and for personal use are of interest with respect to serving the client populations for JTPA and ES/UI. One question that addresses this issue asked respondents how often they read or used information from four different types of literacy materials on the job — reports or journal articles, forms, letters, and diagrams or schematics. As shown in Table 5.5, the most frequently used material on the job by JTPA applicants was forms, with 47 percent of the applicants reporting that they use forms every day or a few times a week. About 25 percent of the applicants report using each of the other types of materials with that frequency.

| Table 5.5 | Distributions of JTPA Applicants and ES/UI Participants Reporting How Often They Use Literacy Materials on the Job* |

	n	Weighted N	Every Day	A Few Times a Week	Once a Week	Less than Once a Week	Never
JTPA							
Reports/Journal Articles	2,146	957,958	18.0 (1.1)	10.4 (0.9)	7.9 (0.9)	9.7 (1.4)	54.1 (2.0)
Forms	2,143	957,489	37.9 (2.2)	9.3 (1.0)	8.4 (0.9)	8.7 (0.9)	35.6 (1.9)
Letters	2,143	955,657	13.4 (1.4)	11.8 (1.6)	8.1 (0.9)	11.4 (1.7)	55.3 (2.2)
Diagrams/Schematics	2,146	963,717	17.7 (1.3)	7.5 (0.8)	6.6 (0.8)	10.4 (1.0)	57.7 (1.6)
ES/UI							
Reports/Journal Articles	3,138	18,070,265	31.9 (1.5)	13.7 (0.8)	8.5 (0.4)	11.5 (0.9)	34.5 (1.7)
Forms	3,129	18,014,144	55.5 (2.8)	9.6 (0.8)	6.5 (1.0)	6.6 (0.7)	21.9 (1.8)
Letters	3,128	17,999,850	25.9 (1.8)	14.7 (0.9)	8.3 (0.5)	13.2 (1.1)	37.9 (2.2)
Diagrams/Schematics	3,127	18,030,026	23.0 (2.6)	9.9 (0.9)	8.2 (0.9)	11.2 (0.8)	47.7 (2.6)

*The numbers in parentheses are estimated standard errors.

A greater percentage of the ES/UI population report using the four types of materials every day or a few times a week as compared with the JTPA population. As can be seen in Table 5.5, the ES/UI participants also use forms more frequently than other materials, with 65 percent reporting that they use forms every day or a few times a week. This frequency is also reported by 45 percent of the participants for reports, by 40 percent for letters, and by 33 percent for diagrams.

Writing Activities on the Job

Respondents were asked how often they write or fill out memos or business letters, reports, forms, and bills or invoices on the job. As can be seen in Table 5.6, the greatest percentage of JTPA applicants report that they fill out forms (44 percent) every day or a few times a week, followed by reports (30 percent), memos (21 percent), and bills (20 percent).

A greater percentage of ES/UI participants than JTPA applicants report they write up or fill out the four kinds of documents frequently. As shown in Table 5.6, 58 percent of the ES/UI participants report filling out forms every day or a few times a week, followed by 41 percent for reports, 32 percent for bills, and 38 percent for memos.

Table 5.6	Distributions of JTPA Applicants and ES/UI Participants Reporting How Often They Engage in Writing on the Job*						
	n	Weighted N	Every Day	A Few Times a Week	Once a Week	Less than Once a Week	Never
JTPA							
Memos/Letters	2,144	955,459	14.3 (1.0)	7.0 (0.9)	4.1 (1.0)	8.2 (0.7)	66.5 (1.9)
Reports	2,137	951,561	23.6 (1.5)	6.1 (1.1)	6.8 (0.5)	8.0 (1.0)	55.5 (1.7)
Forms	2,141	956,090	36.8 (2.1)	7.3 (0.8)	6.6 (0.8)	8.2 (0.7)	41.1 (2.2)
Bills/Invoices	2,141	954,724	14.4 (0.8)	6.0 (0.6)	4.6 (0.7)	8.1 (1.2)	66.9 (1.6)
ES/UI							
Memos/Letters	3,137	18,033,334	25.0 (1.9)	12.5 (0.9)	7.4 (0.7)	9.6 (0.8)	45.6 (2.8)
Reports	3,136	18,040,949	31.4 (1.4)	10.2 (0.8)	11.4 (0.6)	11.3 (1.3)	35.7 (1.7)
Forms	3,132	18,026,922	47.7 (2.4)	10.7 (0.6)	8.7 (0.9)	6.6 (0.5)	26.3 (2.1)
Bills/Invoices	3,130	18,011,281	21.3 (1.4)	10.4 (0.9)	7.4 (0.8)	9.4 (0.9)	51.5 (1.9)

*The numbers in parentheses are estimated standard errors.

Frequency of Newspaper Reading

As shown by data from the young adult literacy assessment,[1] one important indication of literacy practice is the frequency with which people report reading a newspaper. Table 5.7 shows the frequencies with which the JTPA population reports reading a newspaper in English. The table indicates that about 90 percent of the applicants report reading a newspaper at least once a week and only about 3 percent report never reading a newspaper. There do not seem to be any significant differences by race/ethnicity in the frequency of reported newspaper reading, except that a greater percentage of Hispanic than White applicants report that they never read a newspaper in English. Respondent's level of education, however, does seem to be associated with the frequency of reported newspaper reading. For example, only 29 percent of those with less than a high school education report reading a newspaper

Table 5.7	Frequency of Reported Newspaper Reading for JTPA Applicants by Race/Ethnicity, Level of Education, Age, and Labor Force Status*

	n	Weighted N	Every Day	A Few Times a Week	Once a Week	Less than Once a Week	Never
TOTAL	2,495	1,098,167	44.5 (2.4)	32.7 (1.6)	14.4 (1.8)	5.6 (0.8)	2.9 (0.7)
RACE/ETHNICITY							
White	1,554	760,336	43.5 (2.2)	33.6 (1.8)	15.0 (2.0)	6.0 (1.1)	1.9 (0.4)
Black	661	230,074	45.2 (5.2)	32.3 (4.3)	13.3 (3.8)	4.2 (0.7)	5.0 (2.3)
Hispanic	159	64,912	54.9 (5.7)	23.6 (4.5)	10.6 (2.7)	3.8 (1.8)	7.1 (2.6)
LEVEL OF EDUCATION							
0-8 Years	175	64,728	29.0 (4.0)	33.0 (6.3)	18.1 (5.2)	9.0 (1.6)	11.0 (4.0)
9-12 Years	704	302,094	40.6 (3.5)	32.0 (1.8)	17.5 (2.9)	4.6 (1.1)	5.2 (1.5)
H.S. Dip. or GED	1,044	484,560	45.0 (2.6)	33.9 (2.4)	13.7 (2.1)	6.5 (1.2)	0.9 (0.3)
Some Postsecondary	440	184,203	51.1 (3.7)	30.1 (4.0)	12.2 (2.4)	4.6 (1.0)	2.0 (1.2)
College Degree	130	61,480	55.9 (5.2)	32.1 (4.9)	7.2 (3.5)	3.7 (1.8)	1.1 (0.7)
AGE							
16-20	489	185,317	36.0 (3.0)	35.4 (2.8)	16.7 (3.8)	7.2 (1.5)	4.8 (1.4)
21-25	484	213,714	42.4 (4.1)	31.9 (3.9)	14.9 (1.8)	8.0 (1.5)	2.8 (1.1)
26-31	504	233,703	42.1 (4.5)	38.4 (4.0)	14.4 (2.3)	3.6 (0.9)	1.5 (0.7)
32-45	733	340,218	45.1 (2.3)	33.3 (3.3)	13.0 (2.3)	6.1 (1.4)	2.5 (1.1)
46+	259	115,018	66.5 (5.5)	17.0 (4.7)	11.4 (3.3)	1.7 (0.8)	3.4 (2.5)
LABOR FORCE STATUS							
Employed	492	241,746	52.0 (3.3)	27.2 (3.2)	12.2 (2.9)	6.2 (1.6)	2.4 (0.7)
Not Employed	827	352,733	45.2 (3.1)	36.5 (3.3)	11.5 (1.7)	4.9 (1.2)	2.0 (0.7)
Out of Labor Force	1,176	503,688	40.3 (3.4)	32.7 (1.6)	17.4 (2.8)	5.9 (1.0)	3.7 (1.2)

*The numbers in parentheses are estimated standard errors.

---

[1] I. S. Kirsch, A. Jungeblut, and D. A. Rock. (1988). *Reading newspapers: The practices of America's young adults.* (Princeton, NJ: Educational Testing Service.)

daily compared with a range of 41 to 56 percent of those with higher levels of education. Similarly, a greater percentage of those over the age of 45 read a newspaper daily as compared with those aged 45 and under.

About 90 percent of the ES/UI population also report reading a newspaper at least once a week, as seen from Table 5.8. As with the JTPA applicants, there is a difference in reported frequency of newspaper reading between White and Hispanic participants; in the case of ES/UI, however, the difference appears with respect to daily reading (instead of not reading), with about 58 percent of the White participants and about 42 percent of the Hispanic participants reporting daily newspaper reading. For the ES/UI population, there is also an association between level of education and frequency of reported newspaper reading. With respect to daily newspaper reading, the most significant difference occurs, however, between those with less than or some high school and those with at least some postsecondary

Table 5.8	Frequency of Reported Newspaper Reading for ES/UI Participants by Race/Ethnicity, Level of Education, Age, and Labor Force Status*						
	n	Weighted N	Every Day	A Few Times a Week	Once a Week	Less than Once a Week	Never
TOTAL	3,273	18,888,425	53.5 (2.3)	28.2 (0.8)	10.9 (1.4)	5.4 (0.6)	2.1 (0.5)
RACE/ETHNICITY							
White	2,393	11,891,452	57.6 (2.2)	25.9 (1.4)	10.5 (1.3)	4.8 (0.7)	1.3 (0.3)
Black	375	2,189,197	50.7 (4.0)	29.6 (1.4)	10.4 (1.9)	7.2 (2.6)	2.0 (0.8)
Hispanic	384	3,824,079	41.5 (2.2)	34.3 (2.7)	12.6 (3.5)	6.5 (1.4)	5.0 (1.5)
LEVEL OF EDUCATION							
0-8 Years	120	511,432	37.6 (6.0)	22.5 (8.8)	15.0 (4.6)	8.6 (4.2)	16.3 (7.5)
9-12 Years	500	2,941,253	44.7 (3.9)	28.9 (2.5)	15.2 (2.4)	8.7 (1.6)	2.5 (0.8)
H.S. Dip. or GED	1,279	6,681,481	52.6 (2.6)	28.0 (1.5)	11.3 (1.8)	6.3 (1.2)	1.8 (0.7)
Some Postsecondary	860	5,149,103	54.8 (2.3)	31.5 (1.4)	7.7 (0.9)	4.4 (1.1)	1.6 (0.6)
College Degree	511	3,582,636	62.7 (3.4)	23.7 (2.5)	10.6 (1.4)	2.4 (1.0)	0.7 (0.7)
AGE							
16-20	314	1,845,836	45.9 (4.2)	37.0 (2.4)	9.5 (3.7)	5.5 (1.7)	2.1 (0.9)
21-25	616	3,418,336	42.0 (3.9)	34.1 (2.7)	15.0 (2.2)	7.5 (1.2)	1.4 (0.8)
26-31	727	4,146,004	43.8 (3.4)	34.4 (1.1)	12.0 (2.0)	5.8 (1.4)	4.0 (2.0)
32-45	1,059	6,109,941	57.8 (2.0)	24.2 (1.2)	10.7 (1.4)	5.8 (0.7)	1.6 (0.5)
46+	544	3,289,378	73.4 (3.5)	16.8 (2.2)	6.4 (2.5)	2.2 (0.9)	1.2 (0.6)
LABOR FORCE STATUS							
Employed	1,297	7,145,732	51.8 (2.9)	29.6 (2.9)	10.4 (1.7)	6.0 (0.8)	2.4 (0.8)
Not Employed	1,126	6,404,895	59.0 (2.9)	25.8 (2.0)	9.4 (1.9)	4.9 (1.5)	1.0 (0.3)
Out of Labor Force	850	5,337,797	49.1 (2.0)	29.3 (2.4)	13.3 (1.2)	5.4 (1.3)	2.9 (1.4)

*The numbers in parentheses are estimated standard errors.

education. In addition, the percentages of participants who report never reading a newspaper decreases from 16 percent for those with less than high school to about 1 percent for those with college degrees. There also appears to be more of an association between age and reported frequency of newspaper reading for the ES/UI population than for JTPA. The percentage for daily newspaper reading increases significantly from about 44 percent for those aged 26 to 31 to about 58 percent for those aged 32 to 45, and then to 73 percent for those over age 45.

● SELF-PERCEPTIONS ABOUT LITERACY SKILLS

Adequacy of Literacy Skills

JTPA applicants and ES/UI participants who indicated they had worked were asked whether they felt their reading, writing, and mathematics skills were good enough for their jobs. Table 5.9 shows percentages of "yes" and "no" responses in each of the three skill areas for the JTPA population, that is, of those who feel that their skills were adequate for their jobs and of those who feel that their skills were not adequate. With few exceptions, at least 90 percent of the applicants report that they thought their skills were adequate in each of the three areas. As might be expected, the exceptions with respect to education level are those with zero to eight years of education for all three skill areas as well as those with nine to 12 years of education for writing and mathematics. Surprisingly, however, more than 75 percent of these groups indicate that their skill levels were adequate. It would follow that significantly greater percentages of applicants with less than a high school diploma or GED would indicate that both their writing and mathematics skills were inadequate for their job, as compared with those who attained a high school diploma or GED and above. The only significant difference with respect to age is that the percentage of applicants over the age of 45 who feel their writing skills are adequate is lower as compared with 26- to 45-year-olds. In addition, a greater percentage of those out of the work force feel that their mathematics skills are inadequate when compared with applicants who are employed.

As shown in Table 5.10 with few exceptions, at least 90 percent of the ES/UI participants report that their reading, writing, and mathematics skills are adequate for their job. For the ES/UI population, the percentages for the same groups and skill areas as in the JTPA population fall below 90 percent — that is, those with zero to eight years of education for all three skill areas and those with nine to 12 years of education for writing and mathematics. In contrast to the JTPA population, however, less than 75 percent of those with zero to eight years of education feel that their skills were adequate in all three skill areas.

Table 5.9

Distributions of JTPA Applicants' Self-Perceptions About Their Skills by Race/Ethnicity, Level of Education, Age, and Labor Force Status*

	Reading				Writing			
	n	Weighted N	Yes	No	n	Weighted N	Yes	No
TOTAL	2,157	974,973	96.2 (0.7)	3.1 (0.6)	2,158	973,915	93.0 (0.8)	5.5 (0.8)
RACE/ETHNICITY								
White	1,363	690,623	96.5 (0.8)	2.7 (0.6)	1,364	691,031	93.6 (0.7)	4.8 (0.8)
Black	541	185,636	96.1 (1.6)	3.5 (1.6)	540	184,043	93.5 (2.0)	5.9 (2.1)
Hispanic	146	60,118	92.3 (2.6)	7.3 (2.5)	147	60,246	87.3 (2.8)	9.2 (2.8)
LEVEL OF EDUCATION								
0-8 Years	134	52,976	84.4 (5.1)	14.4 (5.1)	135	52,311	77.4 (5.7)	16.1 (6.2)
9-12 Years	539	238,209	93.8 (1.1)	5.8 (1.1)	540	238,366	88.8 (2.1)	8.4 (1.6)
H.S. Dip. or GED	942	444,698	97.7 (0.6)	1.8 (0.5)	940	443,859	96.0 (0.7)	3.2 (0.7)
Some Postsecondary	414	177,347	98.9 (1.1)	0.0 (0.0)	415	177,636	95.3 (1.4)	4.3 (1.4)
College Degree	126	60,640	97.4 (1.5)	1.6 (1.0)	126	60,640	94.6 (3.6)	5.4 (3.6)
AGE								
16-20	287	113,288	96.6 (1.5)	2.8 (1.4)	287	112,501	91.3 (3.1)	4.1 (1.6)
21-25	428	191,866	96.2 (1.4)	2.0 (0.9)	428	191,866	93.1 (1.7)	5.3 (1.4)
26-31	468	219,420	96.1 (1.4)	3.7 (1.4)	467	219,278	95.6 (1.3)	3.9 (1.4)
32-45	713	333,195	97.3 (0.8)	2.2 (0.7)	713	332,985	93.6 (1.2)	5.5 (1.3)
46+	248	111,114	93.0 (2.8)	7.0 (2.8)	250	111,197	88.3 (2.1)	10.2 (2.2)
LABOR FORCE STATUS								
Employed	440	221,959	97.2 (0.9)	2.4 (0.8)	440	221,959	93.0 (1.6)	5.7 (1.8)
Not Employed	770	336,083	97.1 (0.7)	1.7 (0.5)	771	336,656	93.6 (1.4)	5.3 (1.3)
Out of Labor Force	947	416,931	95.0 (1.2)	4.7 (1.1)	947	415,301	92.6 (0.8)	5.5 (0.8)

	Mathematics			
	n	Weighted N	Yes	No
TOTAL	2,158	973,981	90.3 (0.9)	8.1 (0.9)
RACE/ETHNICITY				
White	1,365	691,211	89.6 (1.2)	8.4 (1.2)
Black	539	183,929	92.3 (2.1)	7.1 (2.2)
Hispanic	147	60,246	92.4 (2.6)	6.0 (2.2)
LEVEL OF EDUCATION				
0-8 Years	135	52,311	75.8 (5.4)	23.4 (4.9)
9-12 Years	539	237,935	85.7 (2.0)	11.5 (1.9)
H.S. Dip. or GED	941	444,356	92.8 (0.9)	6.1 (0.8)
Some Postsecondary	415	177,636	94.1 (1.7)	4.6 (1.5)
College Degree	126	60,640	93.3 (2.7)	5.5 (2.9)
AGE				
16-20	287	112,501	87.6 (3.4)	10.1 (3.4)
21-25	428	191,866	91.3 (2.1)	6.7 (2.0)
26-31	467	218,988	90.3 (2.3)	7.1 (1.9)
32-45	713	333,340	90.9 (1.4)	8.2 (1.1)
46+	250	111,197	89.7 (2.1)	9.9 (2.1)
LABOR FORCE STATUS				
Employed	438	221,370	94.2 (1.4)	4.7 (1.4)
Not Employed	770	336,542	91.1 (1.5)	7.2 (1.2)
Out of Labor Force	950	416,069	87.6 (1.6)	10.6 (1.5)

*The numbers in parentheses are estimated standard errors.

Table 5.10

Distributions of ES/UI Participants' Self-Perceptions About Their Skills
by Race/Ethnicity, Level of Education, Age, and Labor Force Status*

	Reading				Writing			
	n	Weighted N	Yes	No	n	Weighted N	Yes	No
TOTAL	3,141	18,090,159	95.6 (0.9)	4.0 (0.8)	3,140	18,065,145	90.6 (0.8)	8.2 (0.7)
RACE/ETHNICITY								
White	2,309	11,549,283	97.0 (0.5)	2.7 (0.4)	2,309	11,539,004	92.1 (0.8)	6.9 (0.8)
Black	351	2,063,222	96.5 (1.6)	3.5 (1.6)	351	2,063,222	93.8 (1.2)	5.9 (1.1)
Hispanic	367	3,562,496	90.7 (3.7)	8.1 (3.0)	366	3,547,761	85.6 (5.9)	11.8 (4.7)
LEVEL OF EDUCATION								
0-8 Years	117	503,275	62.7 (9.8)	31.3 (9.2)	117	503,275	54.7 (4.5)	40.2 (2.6)
9-12 Years	461	2,598,657	92.7 (2.4)	6.8 (2.4)	461	2,598,657	86.9 (3.4)	12.1 (3.4)
H.S. Dip. or GED	1,231	6,451,727	96.1 (0.8)	3.8 (0.8)	1,232	6,441,438	91.1 (1.5)	8.1 (1.4)
Some Postsecondary	825	4,950,425	98.1 (0.7)	1.2 (0.6)	823	4,935,699	93.9 (1.3)	5.0 (1.0)
College Degree	504	3,563,557	97.7 (1.1)	2.3 (1.1)	504	3,563,557	93.1 (2.0)	5.8 (2.3)
AGE								
16-20	247	1,377,248	99.6 (0.1)	0.2 (0.2)	247	1,377,248	94.7 (1.2)	4.6 (1.3)
21-25	583	3,255,300	95.9 (1.8)	3.5 (1.7)	582	3,256,068	93.5 (1.5)	5.9 (1.4)
26-31	716	4,121,137	95.5 (1.0)	4.4 (1.0)	715	4,106,402	90.9 (1.4)	8.4 (1.6)
32-45	1,044	6,005,148	95.3 (1.6)	4.4 (1.7)	1,045	6,007,371	87.7 (1.4)	10.5 (1.5)
46+	539	3,265,128	94.4 (1.6)	4.7 (1.4)	539	3,251,857	90.7 (1.7)	7.7 (1.2)
LABOR FORCE STATUS								
Employed	1,262	6,985,495	97.2 (0.9)	2.7 (0.9)	1,264	6,989,941	91.5 (1.2)	7.1 (1.2)
Not Employed	1,099	6,260,871	95.6 (1.1)	4.3 (1.1)	1,097	6,244,643	90.2 (1.2)	9.1 (1.0)
Out of Labor Force	780	4,843,793	93.2 (1.4)	5.5 (1.5)	779	4,830,560	89.6 (1.7)	8.8 (1.4)

	Mathematics			
	n	Weighted N	Yes	No
TOTAL	3,139	18,077,173	91.9 (0.8)	7.1 (0.9)
RACE/ETHNICITY				
White	2,309	11,545,439	92.9 (0.8)	6.2 (0.9)
Black	351	2,063,222	93.4 (1.7)	5.4 (1.5)
Hispanic	366	3,557,926	87.7 (3.9)	10.9 (3.0)
LEVEL OF EDUCATION				
0-8 Years	117	503,275	66.7 (5.9)	27.4 (5.4)
9-12 Years	461	2,598,657	83.5 (3.5)	15.2 (3.5)
H.S. Dip. or GED	1,230	6,443,579	92.1 (1.5)	7.0 (1.5)
Some Postsecondary	825	4,950,158	95.2 (0.9)	3.6 (1.2)
College Degree	503	3,558,987	96.7 (1.0)	3.3 (1.0)
AGE				
16-20	247	1,377,248	92.8 (2.5)	3.8 (1.9)
21-25	584	3,259,304	92.9 (2.4)	6.7 (2.4)
26-31	715	4,116,566	92.2 (1.2)	7.6 (1.2)
32-45	1,041	5,990,505	90.8 (1.5)	8.1 (1.4)
46+	540	3,267,351	92.2 (2.5)	6.4 (2.1)
LABOR FORCE STATUS				
Employed	1,262	6,981,098	93.6 (0.9)	5.7 (0.8)
Not Employed	1,097	6,252,549	91.9 (1.1)	7.5 (1.1)
Out of Labor Force	780	4,843,526	89.6 (1.4)	8.5 (1.8)

*The numbers in parentheses are estimated standard errors.

Quality of Job with Respect to Additional Training

For this survey, perhaps more important than the perceived adequacy of skills for one's job is whether or not respondents feel they could get a job or a better job if they received additional training in reading or writing and in mathematics. As shown in Table 5.11, 67 percent of the JTPA applicants feel they could get a job (or a better job) if they received additional training in reading or writing, and 79 percent feel that way with respect to additional training in mathematics. It is apparent from the table that, when compared with White applicants, significantly more Black and Hispanic applicants feel they could get a (better) job if they received training in both reading or writing and in mathematics. Significant differences also occur with respect to level of education. When compared with those who earned a high school diploma or a GED, significantly larger percentages of applicants with less than or some high school education feel they could get a (better) job if they received additional training in reading or writing; and, in turn, the percentages of those with a high school diploma or GED and with some postsecondary education are significantly higher than the percentage for college graduates. These trends are also evident with respect to perceptions about additional training in mathematics, except that the difference

| Table 5.11 | Distributions of JTPA Applicants Regarding Relationship Between (Better) Job and Training by Race/Ethnicity, Level of Education, Age, and Labor Force Status* |

	Reading or Writing English				Mathematics			
	n	Weighted N	Yes	No	n	Weighted N	Yes	No
TOTAL	2,479	1,091,984	66.6 (2.2)	33.4 (2.2)	2,475	1,089,072	79.3 (2.0)	20.7 (2.0)
RACE/ETHNICITY								
White	1,542	754,963	60.1 (2.0)	39.9 (2.0)	1,538	752,296	75.4 (2.1)	24.6 (2.1)
Black	661	230,133	82.0 (4.3)	18.0 (4.3)	659	229,460	89.2 (2.1)	10.8 (2.1)
Hispanic	156	64,305	81.6 (4.2)	18.4 (4.2)	158	64,731	83.8 (3.2)	16.2 (3.2)
LEVEL OF EDUCATION								
0-8 Years	175	64,817	86.5 (2.6)	13.5 (2.6)	175	64,817	85.7 (4.1)	14.3 (4.1)
9-12 Years	696	299,399	79.2 (3.0)	20.8 (3.0)	696	297,444	86.8 (2.6)	13.2 (2.6)
H.S. Dip. or GED	1,036	481,049	61.0 (3.6)	39.0 (3.6)	1,034	480,737	78.4 (2.8)	21.6 (2.8)
Some Postsecondary	440	184,137	63.3 (2.5)	36.7 (2.5)	441	184,318	80.6 (2.8)	19.4 (2.8)
College Degree	130	61,480	37.2 (8.2)	62.8 (8.2)	127	60,654	38.8 (9.3)	61.2 (9.3)
AGE								
16-20	485	184,343	74.4 (3.4)	25.6 (3.4)	485	184,837	82.2 (1.8)	17.8 (1.8)
21-25	481	213,144	67.6 (2.7)	32.4 (2.7)	479	211,444	80.0 (3.2)	20.0 (3.2)
26-31	498	230,405	62.4 (3.4)	37.6 (3.4)	499	228,447	80.6 (2.8)	19.4 (2.8)
32-45	730	339,767	66.4 (4.1)	33.6 (4.1)	726	338,851	78.2 (3.9)	21.8 (3.9)
46+	257	113,723	59.5 (2.8)	40.5 (2.8)	258	114,893	73.6 (2.7)	26.4 (2.7)
LABOR FORCE STATUS								
Employed	486	238,507	65.1 (3.5)	34.9 (3.5)	489	240,183	79.8 (2.8)	20.2 (2.8)
Not Employed	826	352,518	62.1 (3.0)	37.9 (3.0)	822	351,728	72.8 (3.0)	27.2 (3.0)
Out of Labor Force	1,167	500,959	70.5 (3.0)	29.5 (3.0)	1,164	497,161	83.7 (2.0)	16.3 (2.0)

*The numbers in parentheses are estimated standard errors.

between those with less than high school and those with a high school diploma or GED is not significant. When labor force status is considered with respect to both reading or writing and mathematics skills, a significantly greater percentage of those out of the labor force than those unemployed feel that they could get a job if they received additional training.

Of particular note when considering the kinds of training to implement for DOL clients is that for the total JTPA population a larger percentage feel they could get a (better) job if they received additional training in mathematics. This is the same regardless of age or labor force status. There are, however, no significant differences with respect to the two kinds of training for Black and Hispanic JTPA applicants and for those at either extreme of educational attainment — those with zero to eight years of education and those reporting a college degree.

When compared with the JTPA population, a lower percentage of ES/UI participants feel they would get a (better) job if they received additional training in reading or writing (57 percent) and in mathematics (69 percent), as shown in Table 5.12. As with the JTPA applicants, a significantly larger percentage of Black and Hispanic ES/UI participants than White participants feel that they could get a

Table 5.12	Distributions of ES/UI Participants Regarding Relationship Between (Better) Job and Training by Race/Ethnicity, Level of Education, Age, and Labor Force Status*

	Reading or Writing English				Mathematics			
	n	Weighted N	Yes	No	n	Weighted N	Yes	No
TOTAL	3,253	18,733,323	57.3 (2.9)	42.7 (2.9)	3,251	18,727,928	69.4 (2.5)	30.6 (2.5)
RACE/ETHNICITY								
White	2,382	11,848,101	44.3 (2.9)	55.7 (2.9)	2,381	11,846,455	60.5 (2.5)	39.5 (2.5)
Black	373	2,183,531	76.3 (2.1)	23.7 (2.1)	373	2,183,531	82.6 (2.2)	17.4 (2.2)
Hispanic	377	3,729,256	83.0 (5.0)	17.0 (5.0)	377	3,730,078	89.7 (4.8)	10.3 (4.8)
LEVEL OF EDUCATION								
0-8 Years	119	509,013	92.8 (3.7)	7.2 (3.7)	119	509,013	87.2 (7.0)	12.8 (7.0)
9-12 Years	495	2,859,040	75.0 (3.7)	25.0 (3.7)	497	2,865,877	83.5 (3.3)	16.5 (3.3)
H.S. Dip. or GED	1,269	6,642,973	61.7 (2.3)	38.3 (2.3)	1,267	6,652,693	75.1 (1.9)	24.9 (1.9)
Some Postsecondary	855	5,103,388	52.8 (2.4)	47.2 (2.4)	855	5,103,868	69.6 (2.8)	30.4 (2.8)
College Degree	512	3,596,390	36.3 (5.2)	63.7 (5.2)	510	3,573,958	44.4 (2.7)	55.6 (2.7)
AGE								
16-20	310	1,767,895	68.4 (5.9)	31.6 (5.9)	311	1,770,460	84.2 (2.6)	15.8 (2.6)
21-25	614	3,403,138	69.6 (5.1)	30.4 (5.1)	614	3,406,135	80.6 (4.1)	19.4 (4.1)
26-31	720	4,116,753	56.7 (3.4)	43.3 (3.4)	721	4,132,507	71.4 (3.1)	28.6 (3.1)
32-45	1,054	6,077,483	52.8 (2.6)	47.2 (2.6)	1,050	6,048,818	65.9 (2.5)	34.1 (2.5)
46+	541	3,283,592	46.5 (3.6)	53.5 (3.6)	542	3,287,864	53.3 (3.1)	46.7 (3.1)
LABOR FORCE STATUS								
Employed	1,293	7,108,380	53.1 (3.2)	46.9 (3.2)	1,290	7,094,265	66.3 (2.8)	33.7 (2.8)
Not Employed	1,117	6,371,874	56.0 (2.0)	44.0 (2.0)	1,118	6,378,640	69.2 (2.0)	30.8 (2.0)
Out of Labor Force	843	5,253,068	64.4 (5.1)	35.6 (5.1)	843	5,255,022	73.6 (3.8)	26.4 (3.8)

*The numbers in parentheses are estimated standard errors.

(better) job if they received additional training in both reading or writing and in mathematics. When participants are compared by level of education, the percentages of participants who feel that training in reading or writing would be a help decrease significantly as the level of education increases. There is no similar category-by-category decrease with mathematics training as there is with reading or writing; however, a significantly higher percentage of participants with some high school feel that such training would help than do those with a high school diploma or GED. In turn, a significantly greater percentage of those with a high school diploma or GED and some postsecondary than college graduates feel that additional mathematics training would assist them in getting a (better) job. The ES/UI population does not show the significant differences between those who are out of the labor force and those who are unemployed that are evident for the JTPA population.

Consistent with the trend for JTPA, a significantly larger percentage of the total ES/UI population report that additional mathematics training would assist them in getting a (better) job (69 percent) compared with the percentage who feel additional training in reading or writing would help (57 percent). In addition, while a larger percentage of White and Black ES/UI participants indicate that mathematics training would be helpful, the difference is not significant among Hispanic participants. Similarly, a larger percentage of those who report a high school diploma or GED and some postsecondary education also indicate that mathematics would be helpful, as do a larger percentage of those ES/UI participants who are employed or unemployed. Again, the difference is not significant among those who were out of the labor force.

Help Received for Literacy Activities

Another indication of whether people feel their literacy skills are adequate is the frequency with which others help them with various literacy activities. Respondents were asked how frequently family members or friends helped them with filling out forms, explaining articles or other types of written information, dealing with agencies, companies, medical personnel, etc., and writing notes and letters. As can be seen in Table 5.13, over 80 percent of the total JTPA population indicate they never receive help or receive help only once or twice a year for each of the four activities. Although not shown in this table, this rate remains similar regardless of race/ethnicity, with the percentages ranging from 87 to 91, 81 to 86, and 81 to 87 for White, Black, and Hispanic applicants, respectively. Some differences in the rates do occur when the JTPA population is broken down by level of education and age. For all the activities except writing letters, greater percentages of those with less than a high school education and those aged 16 to 20 receive help more often.

Table 5.13

Distributions of JTPA Applicants and ES/UI Participants
Reporting How Often They Receive Help with Literacy Activities*

	n	Weighted N	Daily	Weekly	Every Month	Once or Twice a Year	Never
JTPA							
Filling Out Forms	2,483	1,092,157	1.9 (0.5)	4.5 (0.8)	7.1 (0.5)	24.4 (1.4)	62.1 (1.6)
Reading Written Info.	2,479	1,088,414	4.2 (0.6)	5.5 (0.7)	4.3 (0.4)	12.7 (0.9)	73.3 (1.4)
Dealing with Agencies	2,478	1,088,426	2.5 (0.5)	2.7 (0.5)	8.3 (0.9)	26.3 (1.1)	60.3 (1.4)
Writing Letters	2,480	1,089,551	3.1 (0.5)	4.1 (0.6)	3.2 (0.5)	10.3 (0.7)	79.2 (1.1)
ES/UI							
Filling Out Forms	3,263	18,789,008	1.9 (0.3)	2.6 (0.5)	4.3 (0.8)	19.3 (1.1)	71.9 (1.2)
Reading Written Info.	3,261	18,794,753	2.6 (0.6)	3.6 (0.5)	2.9 (0.3)	10.9 (0.7)	80.0 (1.3)
Dealing with Agencies	3,263	18,797,718	1.1 (0.3)	3.3 (0.7)	6.4 (0.9)	28.2 (2.3)	61.0 (2.1)
Writing Letters	3,259	18,799,904	1.5 (0.5)	3.1 (0.5)	5.3 (0.5)	8.4 (0.7)	81.7 (1.0)

*The numbers in parentheses are estimated standard errors.

Generally, about 90 percent of the ES/UI participants report that they never receive help or receive help only once or twice a year for each of the four activities, as can also be seen in Table 5.13. Over 90 percent of the White participants, 85 to 90 percent of the Black participants, and 84 to 87 percent of the Hispanic participants indicate that they receive infrequent or no help for each of the four activities. A greater percentage of those with less than a high school education receive help more frequently than those with the other levels of education. As with the JTPA population, a greater percentage of those aged 16 to 20 receive help more often as compared with the other age groups for all activities except letter writing. For both the ES/UI and JTPA populations, there are no major differences by labor force status. (More detailed tabular information can be found in Appendix E of the Final Report).

● **SUMMARY**

With respect to activities related to civic and political behavior, well over half of the JTPA and ES/UI participants (58 and 62 percent, respectively) report being registered to vote. Of those individuals registered, some 60 and 64 percent of the JTPA and ES/UI populations report that they have voted in an election. As noted in Section 4 with variables related to education, race/ethnicity is not a salient variable with respect to being registered to vote among JTPA applicants. However, percentages increase for each increasing category of age and educational attainment for both registering and exercising the right to vote. In addition, a significantly smaller percentage of JTPA applicants who report being out of the labor force report that they were registered or had voted.

In contrast, the ES/UI participants show interesting racial/ethnic differences in being registered and voting. As compared with 66 and 46 percent of White and Hispanic participants, respectively, 73 percent of the Black subgroup members report being registered to vote. On the other hand, 73 percent of the White and 68 percent of the Black participants report having voted while the comparable percentage for Hispanic participants is 37. As with JTPA applicants, increases in percentages of individuals registered and voting are related to increases in both age and educational attainment among ES/UI participants. Labor force status was not significantly related for the ES/UI population.

When asked whether they follow public affairs most of the time, some of the time, only now and then, or hardly at all, over 70 percent of both DOL total populations report keeping abreast of public affairs most or some of the time. For both populations, older participants tend to keep more up-to-date on public affairs than do their younger counterparts and the higher the educational attainment the more likely are participants to follow public affairs closely. Again, the results for JTPA applicants show no relationship between racial/ethnic group membership and keeping abreast of public affairs, but there is a significant difference in the percentages of White and Black ES/UI participants who report keeping up with public affairs.

The reported use of literacy skills on the job is important in providing services to both DOL populations. Larger percentages of ES/UI participants report reading or using reports or journal articles, forms, letters, and diagrams or schematics at work than do JTPA applicants — with forms being read or used most frequently by both populations. Similarly, larger percentages of ES/UI than JTPA participants report writing activities related to memos or business letters, reports, forms, and bills — filling out forms was the most frequent writing activity on the job for both populations.

For both DOL groups, approximately 90 percent of the participants report that they read a newspaper in English at least once a week. Daily newspaper reading is associated with educational attainment for both total groups — the higher the level of education, the more likely to report daily reading. The only significant difference related to racial/ethnic group membership for JTPA applicants is that a larger percentage of Hispanic than White respondents report that they never read a newspaper in English; for ES/UI participants, the only significant difference is that a larger percentage of White than Hispanic respondents report reading a newspaper daily. A larger percentage of JTPA applicants over the age of 45 report reading a newspaper daily than do their younger counterparts. On the other hand, there is a steady and significant increase in the percentages of ES/UI participants who report daily newspaper reading by age group, starting with those aged 26 to 31 up through those aged 45 years and older.

JTPA and ES/UI participants were also asked whether they judged their reading, writing, and mathematics skills were adequate for performing their most recent job. In each of the three areas for both DOL populations, rarely are there instances where less than 90 percent of the participants report their skills as adequate for the job. The exceptions for both populations are those with zero to eight years of education in all three areas, and those with nine to 12 years of education in writing and mathematics.

Nevertheless, relatively large percentages of JTPA and ES/UI participants perceive that they could get a job or a better job if their literacy skills were improved. Nearly 80 percent of JTPA and 70 percent of ES/UI respondents report that improvement in mathematics could help them gain employment or a better job. This perception tends to decrease with higher levels of educational attainment. A significantly larger percentage of JTPA applicants who are out of the labor force feel that improved literacy skills would facilitate getting a job than do unemployed JTPA applicants, but this is not apparent in the ES/UI population.

The extent to which individuals receive help from others when faced with various literacy activities is another indication of perceived adequacy of skill. Some 80 to 90 percent of the JTPA and ES/UI populations, respectively, report that they never receive help or receive help only once or twice a year when faced with filling out forms; explaining articles or other types of written information; dealing with agencies, companies, medical personnel, and so forth; and, writing notes and letters. With the exception of writing letters for JTPA applicants, larger percentages of participants in both populations with less than a high school education and aged 16 to 20 receive help more often than their counterparts. No major differences are apparent by labor force status.

SECTION 6

Since the release in 1983 of the seminal report, *A Nation At Risk,*[1] there has been growing concern in America that our education and training system has become inadequate to ensure individual opportunity, to promote growth and prosperity in the economy, and to strengthen our country's ability to compete in an increasingly global economy. These concerns have been fueled by the fact that over the last 20 years or so, there has been a widening gap in earnings between the top 30 percent and bottom 70 percent of wage earners as well as an increase in the percentage of children growing up in poor, one-parent families.[2] Also contributing to these concerns are international educational comparisons, in which our students rank near the bottom — behind children in Europe, Asia, and a number of industrialized countries.[3]

Although our nation's literacy skills have increased dramatically over the last 200 years in response to changing requirements and expanded opportunities, there have also been periods of imbalance — where literacy demands seem to surpass levels of attainment. Today, even though we are a better educated and more literate society

---

[1] National Commission on Excellence in Education. (1983). *A nation at risk: The imperative for educational reform.* (Washington, DC: National Commission on Excellence in Education.)

[2] National Center on Education. (1990). *America's choice: High skills or low wages.* The report of the commission on the skills of the American workforce. (Rochester, NY: National Center on Education.)
R. L. Venezky, C. F. Kaestle, and A. M. Sum. (1987). *The subtle danger: Reflections on the literacy abilities of America's young adults.* (Princeton, NJ: Educational Testing Service.)

[3] H. W. Stevenson and J.W. Stigler. (1992). *The learning gap: Why our schools are failing and what we can learn from Japanese and Chinese education.* (New York, NY: Summit Books.)
A. E. Lapointe, J. M. Askew, and N. A. Mead. (1992). *Learning mathematics* (*Report of the Second International Assessment of Educational Progress*). (Princeton, NJ: Educational Testing Service.)
A. E. Lapointe, J. M. Askew, and N. A. Mead. (1992). *Learning science* (*Report of the Second International Assessment of Educational Progress*). (Princeton, NJ: Educational Testing Service.)

than at any time in our history, we find ourselves in one of these periods of imbalance. The widespread uses of computers and high-speed communications are combining to change the nature and organization of work and learning.

In the past, the strategy to correct these imbalances was to rely on getting increasing numbers of children to stay in school long enough to finish high school. Some have argued that to meet this challenge, we have created a high school system in which there are numerous educational opportunities that meet the needs of a diverse population of students, but where too many of the students are not taught or encouraged to choose wisely among the opportunities or to value learning.[4] As a result, the high school diploma has lost much of its value in representing a core set of knowledge and skills. For example, the data from this DOL assessment show that between 35 and 45 percent of the JTPA and ES/UI populations who report earning a high school diploma or GED demonstrate success on tasks that are limited to locating a single piece of information, entering background information onto a form, or solving a simple, one-step arithmetic problem.

No nation can be expected to produce a highly qualified work force or citizens that are capable of fully participating in a technological society without first providing a strong educational system. If demands encountered by large numbers of individuals in our society were no greater than signing one's name on a form, or locating a single fact in a newspaper or table of employee benefits, then no major changes would be necessary. The disturbing news, however, is that large percentages of both DOL populations demonstrate deficiencies in being able to integrate information across sentences and parts of a document, in being able to generate ideas based on what they have read, in attending to multiple features of information contained in complex displays where they may be required to compare and contrast information, and in sequentially applying arithmetic operations as directed in printed material.

As we move closer to the year 2000, the challenge is not just to find ways of improving the current educational system for future generations of workers, we must also find ways to improve the knowledge and skills of those already in the work force. It is estimated that almost 80 percent of the projected work force for the year 2000 are already employed. As a result, this study raises an important question. Should we seek better ways to teach the current curriculum or do we need to reconsider what is taught and how we teach it?

The authors believe that literacy education and training practices should be broadened both within the formal school program as well as in programs of continuing

---

[4] A. G. Powell, E. Farrar, and D. Cohen. (1985). *The shopping mall high school: Winners and losers in the educational marketplace*. (Boston, MA: Houghton Mifflin.)

adult education. This is the case because the schools are producing future generations of workers and also because the school model for reading instruction is prevalent in many workplace and community education programs. The question is, *how* should existing practices be changed — both behind and beyond the school doors.

Part of the problem appears to rest with the fact that some adult literacy programs aimed at developing comprehension skills are based on elementary school reading models that, for the most part, are restricted to the use of narrative texts. According to one report,[5] the primary emphasis of elementary and middle level reading materials continues to be on the comprehension and enjoyment of fine literature. While instruction should continue to stress the enjoyment and understanding of fiction and poetry, more systematic efforts must be made to develop the skills and strategies associated with success in literacy skills across the full range of printed or written materials associated with home, community, and work environments. Currently, increased recognition is being given to the importance of skill in using these other types of printed information. However, the teaching of these skills and strategies has not yet been fully incorporated into the curriculum.

Given the low literacy levels of many JTPA applicants and ES/UI program participants and the large percentages of high school graduates who demonstrate limited proficiencies (i.e., skills associated with Levels 1 and 2 on each of the three scales), the assessment results suggest that primary emphasis on a single aspect of literacy may not lead to the acquisition of the complex information-processing strategies needed to cope successfully with the broad array of tasks that adults face at work, at home, and in their communities.

In contrast to some programs that emphasize a single aspect of literacy, others have a tendency to focus on the acquisition of skills associated with discrete, "functional" tasks, such as filling out a job application form or using a bus schedule. Frequently, these isolated tasks are referred to as competencies that are then taught in isolation. This approach is also likely to have limited long-term utility for the individual learner. While literacy is not a single skill suited to all types of materials, neither is it an infinite set of skills each associated with a different text or document. Rather, as the analyses in Section 2 show, there appears to be an ordered set of skills and strategies that are called into play to accomplish the range of tasks represented along each of the three literacy scales.

To the extent that the types of tasks used in this assessment are important for access and participation in our society, then the analyses and framework described in

---

[5] R. L. Venezky. (1982). "The origins of the present-day chasm between adult literacy needs and school literacy instruction," *Visible Language*, 16, 113-127.

this report have important implications for the design of instructional materials. As one instance, a taxonomy of document structures that forms the foundation of an instructional system[6] has been generated from the array of tasks used in this and the earlier assessment as well as from a broad review of the technical literature.

In addition to the questions of whether and how to change existing instructional practices is the issue of demand for continuing education and training programs. At this time and for the foreseeable future, there will be increasing pressure on adult programs of continuing education to provide services that successfully meet the needs of individuals demonstrating low-level literacy skills. The GED program is currently filling a portion of the need in relation to high school dropouts — roughly half of each population report studying for the GED. Of these, some 59 and 61 percent of JTPA and ES/UI participants, respectively, report receiving the GED. These figures seem to reflect a need for the introduction of alternative routes for those individuals who pursue but do not complete the GED. Moreover, the fact that around half of the high school dropouts in the DOL populations report not studying for the GED calls into question whether programs in addition to the GED are needed to meet the current literacy needs of these populations.

The results of some cross tabulations of literacy proficiencies with perceived skill in relation to most current job may help illuminate this issue. Of JTPA eligible applicants scoring in Level 1 (0 to 225) on the prose scale, some 81 to 86 percent report that their reading, writing, and mathematics skills were adequate for success in their most current job. On the document scale, the corresponding percentages range from about 80 to 84, while on the quantitative scale the percentages are approximately 76 to 87. The percentages of reported adequacy of skills increases to about 100 percent at higher levels on each of the three literacy scales. The picture is very similar for ES/UI program participants.

Nevertheless, on each of the scales roughly 90 percent of the individuals who score in Level 1 report that improved skills would assist them in obtaining a (better) job. While the percentages decrease at successive levels of proficiency on each of the literacy scales, it is worth noting that significant percentages of program participants at each of the higher levels also believe that continuing to improve their skills, particularly in mathematics, will be associated with better career opportunities.

A third related issue is how to reach and hold individuals who demonstrate and/ or perceive the need for improved literacy skills. The findings of this assessment are clear. Some 40 to 50 percent of the eligible JTPA applicants and ES/UI participants

---

[6] P. B. Mosenthal and I. S. Kirsch. (1989-1991). Understanding Documents. (A column appearing monthly in the issues of the Journal of Reading published between October 1989 and May 1991.)

demonstrate skills that are limited to the ranges defined in this study as Level 1 and Level 2. These are the same individuals who perceive the greatest need for improving their skills. Therefore, the Department of Labor in conjunction with other agencies should work to ensure that adequate literacy programs are available to those program participants who demonstrate limited skill levels.

Unless an attempt is made to upgrade the level of literacy skills of these individuals, their success in job-training programs may be limited, thus hampering their access to the job market. Moreover, for those individuals who do succeed in a job-training program without an increase in their literacy skills, the question remains whether their limited level of proficiency will enable them to avoid future employment difficulties that may arise from projected increases in skill requirements. The most recent round of national employment projections (1990-2005) by the United States Bureau of Labor Statistics indicates that technicians and professional workers will be the most rapidly growing occupation groups, closely followed by managers/administrators. Jobs in the occupational classifications of laborers and operatives are projected to experience the slowest rates of growth — only one-eighth as high as those projected for professional and technical workers.

In the absence of sustained efforts to improve the literacy skills of DOL client groups performing at Levels 1 and 2, the success of DOL-sponsored programs to improve employment or reemployment opportunities, wages, and occupational mobility will, in all likelihood, be severely limited. This is particularly the case for younger participants, those with limited educational experiences, and those whose employment history is limited to unskilled or semi-skilled occupations. Those DOL clients who are able to improve their literacy skills or who already demonstrate higher levels of proficiencies will be in a better position to gain access to the sets of jobs projected to grow more rapidly during the next decade or so. The data from this assessment show that individuals who demonstrate higher levels of literacy skills tend to avoid long periods of unemployment, earn higher wages, and work in higher-level occupations than those individuals who demonstrate skills associated with the lower literacy levels.

America may be coming to understand that it must become a nation of learners. In January 1992, President Bush announced his Job Training 2000 initiative, which is designed to meet the Nation's work force needs into the twenty-first century. Among its many features, this initiative proposes to establish accountability and information systems to ensure a world-class job training system. For example, the Administration proposes that each citizen eligible for federal assistance for education or training have access to a Lifetime Education and Training Account consisting of grants and loans.

Individuals will be encouraged to use the account throughout their lives to continue their education as well as to update their skills.

In the final analysis, it is recognized that many poor, many minorities, and many of those with limited schooling endure distractions and disincentives to learning that prevent them from achieving higher literacy levels. Yet, finding solutions aimed at improving current literacy levels is a necessary step to ensuring individual opportunity, to increasing productivity, and to strengthening the United States' competitiveness in a global society.

Authors' Acknowledgments

The responsibility for this document is ours. Nevertheless, credit, if any should accrue, must be shared with the many individuals who contribute to a project of this size and scope. These individuals range from the consultants who generously gave their thoughts and ideas; to those who designed, printed, and shipped assessment materials; to the JTPA and ES/UI office staff from across the United States who administered the survey; to the 5,778 JTPA applicants and ES/UI participants who responded to the assessment; to those who received, scored, and entered the data and produced the data tape; to those who analyzed the data; and to those who provided expert opinions in interpreting the findings.

Some, because of their particular contribution to this assessment, are named here: Beverly Cisney, Debbie Giannacio, Eugene Johnson, Benjamin King, Mary Michaels, Robert Mislevy, Sheila Moran, Norma Norris, Inge Novatkoski, Katharine Pashley, Donald Rock, Peter Stremic, Lois Worthington, and Kentaro Yamamoto.

Susan Rieger deserves special recognition for her assistance in the training of the JTPA and ES/UI office staff.

We would also like to thank those individuals who provided thoughtful and incisive comments on early drafts of both the final report and this document. Included are: Judy Alamprese, Kent Ashworth, Paul Barton, Evelyn Ganzglass, Karl Haigler, Archie Lapointe, Samuel Messick, Peter Mosenthal, and Andrew Sum.

We appreciate both the support and interest of members of the Department of Labor. First, we would like to thank Gerald Gundersen for his interest and support in this project. We are especially grateful to Mamoru Ishikawa, who in his role as project director facilitated the conduct of the study and demonstrated the professionalism and trust necessary to carry out a project of this type.

We also wish to acknowledge our associate and friend, Jules Goodison, who served as the ETS project codirector and survived the day-to-day experiences of the project and the writing of this report.

Finally, a great deal of expertise was brought to bear in developing this assessment, in scaling and analyzing the data, as well as in reporting the results. We have learned a great deal in the process and hope that we have been able to share some of this knowledge and the accompanying insights in this report.

Irwin Kirsch
Ann Jungeblut
Anne Campbell

Project Staff

Project Advisory Committee	Judith Alamprese, Director of Education and Training, COSMOS Corporation
	Sue Berryman, Director, Institute on Education and the Economy, Teachers College, Columbia University
	Evelyn Ganzglass, Director, Employment and Training Program, National Governors' Association
	Karl Haigler, President, The Salem Company
	Renee Lerche, Manager, Employee Development and External Education Planning, Ford Motor Company
	Lori Strumpf, Project Director, Center for Remediation Design
	Andy Sum, Director, Center for Labor Market Studies, Northeastern University
Project Directors	Jules Goodison
	Irwin Kirsch
Sampling	Benjamin King
	Eugene Johnson
Survey Instruments and Training	Anne Campbell
Field Operations	
Shipping and Receipt Control	Debbie Giannacio
Scoring	Sheila Moran
Data Analysis	Norma Norris
Psychometric/Statistical Analysis	Kentaro Yamamoto
	Donald Rock
	Robert Mislevy